DANCES
OF ENGLAND AND FRANCE
1450 TO 1600

By the same Author

DANCES OF SPAIN AND ITALY FROM 1400 TO 1600

PERSONAL RECOLLECTIONS OF
ARNOLD DOLMETSCH

Illustrated with plates and music

Love leads the Dance in the Garden of Pleasure.

Flemish, 15th Century. British Museum.

DANCES
OF ENGLAND AND FRANCE

FROM 1450 TO 1600

WITH THEIR MUSIC AND AUTHENTIC MANNER
OF PERFORMANCE

BY

MABEL DOLMETSCH

ROUTLEDGE AND KEGAN PAUL LTD
Broadway House. 68–74 Carter Lane
London E.C.4

First published 1949
Second edition 1959

PRINTED IN GREAT BRITAIN BY
LUND HUMPHRIES
LONDON · BRADFORD

To my husband,

ARNOLD DOLMETSCH

and our four children,
Cécile, Nathalie,
Rudolph, and Carl,
this book is affectionately
dedicated.

CONTENTS

ILLUSTRATIONS

INTRODUCTION

ARNOLD DOLMETSCH, whose genius for musical exploration carried him back, during his long years of research, from the nineteenth to the twelfth century, united with his musical curiosity an interest in the sister art of dancing. This led him early in his career to collect a number of treatises, compiled by the great dancing masters of past times, and to perform their music on lute and viol for the delight that it afforded him. He concluded that surely the dances which interpreted such music must partake of the same subtle enchantment. Accordingly he exhibited his rare dancing books to certain accomplished dancers and ballet masters, asking them to study the rules laid down therein and thence to reconstruct these mysterious and forgotten dances.

In this hope he was disappointed, for his dancing acquaintances stared at the pages with bewildered eyes ! An eminent ballet master of the eighteen-nineties said to him, " You just give me the *music* and leave the rest to me ! " After several such disillusionments he allowed the idea to drop for the time being, content to enjoy the music for its own sake ; and there the matter rested for several years. Then one day, while looking on at the impromptu singing and dancing of our own young children, I formed the resolution *myself* to study these ancient treatises and teach the dances to the children. He greeted my project with enthusiasm, recommending me to begin with the books of more recent date and gradually to work back to those of remoter periods. Thus I was eventually able to satisfy his long cherished hopes with a performance of some graceful venitiennes and rigaudons. From then onwards we pursued our research, he assisting me from the musical standpoint, and occasionally helping me to solve some linguistic puzzle, until we had succeeded in reconstructing and performing a hundred or more famous dances and balletti (little suites) of various countries and periods.

It is the result of this practical experience which I now set out to put on record, in such a way as will enable others to perform and enjoy these characteristic and beautiful dances ; the outcome of centuries of art and culture.

After working for some time on the retrogressive plan above described, I came to realize that it was not so much the steps themselves that had altered in the course of time as (1) their style of performance and the way in which they were used and combined ; (2) their method of description ; (3) their nomenclature. The following paragraphs will amplify my meaning.

A French dancing master of the eighteenth century, having survived the Revolution, decided in his old age to publish a collection of French contredanses, in the hope that " les dames " would still be able to rescue the art of dancing from hopeless degeneration. Concerning *steps* he wrote as follows :

" La plupart des jeunes gens vont chez les maîtres de danse pour apprendre tel ou tel pas qu'ils ont vu faire ; mais ils ne savent pas que la danse est (comme tous les autres arts) soumise à des règles générales, et que pour faire un simple changement de jambe, il faut avoir fait des choses encore plus simples ; qu'un pas est composé de plusieurs mouvements, qui ont tous un tac particulier, et qu'on ne peut y mettre l'ensemble, que lorsqu' on en connaît les détails ; que le corps, la tête et les bras ont encore des mouvements qui leur sont propre, et que pour qu'ils puissent agir avec aisance, il faut avoir acquis assez de facilité, pour que le travail des jambes ne porte aucune contr'action au delas de la ceinture, et que le reste du corps soit degagé de toute roideur. Il ne suffit pas de faire des pas ; mais il faut encore danser pour sa Dame, lui presenter la main avec grâce, la conduire à sa place avec douceur, et pour ainsi dire sans qu'elle s'en aperçoive ; faire valoir les moindre choses, et donner à la danse le style élégant dont elle est susceptible.

" Mais comme mon intention n'est pas de faire un cours de danse, je termine, et je dirai seulement, que, grâce au beau Sexe, le bon goût n'est pas encore perdu en France, et que c'est à ce sexe aimable que Terpsychore redevra son empire." [1]

The method employed for describing dance steps differs considerably among the various authors whose works have come down to us. This is fortunate : for thus we find that a comprehensive study of the whole available literature compensates and counteracts the omissions and ambiguities of each individual writer ; and chance slips and errors become manifest.

The nomenclature likewise differs in accordance with each period, country, province, and even district. Where there are no English names, nor anglicized foreign ones available, it will become necessary to employ an assortment of French and Italian terms duly explained. Moreover, where quotations are given, the spelling will in some cases be modernized for the sake of clarity.

---

[1] The title-page of this little book is unfortunately missing.

The Speech of Love persuading men to learn dancing :—

Stanza 60   *Learn then to dance, you that are princes born*
And lawful lords of earthly creatures all.
Imitate them and thereof take no scorn,
(For this new art to them is natural)
And imitate the stars celestial ;
For when pale death your vital twist shall sever,
Your better parts must dance with them forever.

Stanza 61   Thus Love persuades, and all the crown of men
That stands around doth make a murmuring,
As when the wind, loos'd from his hollow den,
Among the trees a gentle bass doth sing,
Or as a brook, through pebbles wandering.
But in their looks they uttered this plain speech :
That they would learn to dance, if Love would teach.

(*Orchestra or a Poem of Dancing.* Sir John Davies, c. 1594)

CHAPTER I

THE BASSE DANSE IN FRANCE

THIS chapter is concerned with the history and bibliography of the Basse Danse. Those whose interest lies principally in learning how to perform the dance may prefer to start with Chapter II.

The dances which flourished at the dawn of the Renaissance were divided into two main types, namely : the Basse Danse and the Haute Danse.

The name Basse Danse signified that, in its performance, the dancer's feet did not leave the ground, whereas the name Haute Danse was applied to all dances which included in their steps, hops, leaps, high jumps, kicks, and stamps.

The Basse Danse (sometimes alluded to as " The Measure " in England) was of a serene and graciously undulating character. We have no record of the exact date at which it came into existence, but at the beginning of the fifteenth century we find it as a firmly established and highly stylized dance which had attached to its service a considerable musical literature of medieval French folk songs. Its well defined and inexorable rules are set forth with remarkable concordance by all French and Italian writers on this subject, throughout the fifteenth and early sixteenth centuries ; i.e. from the unknown author of the *Livre de Basses danses de la Bibliothèque de Bourgogne*[1] (*c.* 1450) to Antonius de Arena the Provençal poet, who published in 1536 a curious but informative discourse on Basses Danses and Branles, couched in Macaronic verse. When, however, we come, in the latter part of the sixteenth century, to the lucid exposition of the Basse Danse in *Orchésographie*, by Thoinot Arbeau, published in 1588, we find certain fundamental modifications in its steps that impose an adaptation of its style and rhythm. This, while adding to their definition, sacrifices something of their subtle grace and sinuosity. Seven Basses Danses are given also in *Il Ballarino*, by Fabritio Caroso, published in Venice, 1581. Some of these, although opening with the characteristic steps and movements, develop in their subsequent figures flourishes (fioretti), hops (zoppetti), and leaps (trabuchetti), which deprive the dance of any title to its ancient name ; two of the examples are presumably of earlier date than the rest for they adhere approximately to the primitive type. These are " Bassa Romana " and " Bassa et Alta ", this latter being a Basse Danse followed by its " Gioiosa " or hopped movement. Cesare Negri in his treatise, *Inventioni*

[1] Supposed to have belonged originally to Marie de Bourgogne, daughter of Charles the Bold, and later the property of her daughter, Marguérite d'Autriche.

DANCES OF ENGLAND AND FRANCE

di Balli, published in Milan in 1604, gives us three Basses Danses which, though grave in character, diverge from the original pattern and contain some " fioretti " and " salti ". These examples complete our record of the long reign of the Basse Danse, styled by the great Italian Masters, " The Queen of Measures."

Let us start our study of the steps by quoting in full a short treatise in English appended to a French Grammar printed by Robert Coplande in 1521, and now in the Bodleian Library.

" Here followeth the manner of dancing of bace dances after the use of France and other places, translated out of French in English by Robert Coplande.[1]

THE MANNER TO DANCE BACE DANCES

1.   For to dance any Bace Dance there behoveth four paces, that is to wit : single, double, reprise, and braule (*branle*). And ye ought first to make reverence toward the lady, and then make 2 singles, 1 double, a reprise, and a braule. And this rule ye ought alway to keep at the beginning, as it is said. And sometime is made 2 singles after the doubles, and before the reprises, and that is done when the measures are perfected. Also when any song or dance is written, R. betokeneth reverence. By SS. double betokeneth 2 single paces, and by d. betokeneth 1 double pace. And if there be ddd. ye ought to make 3 doubles after, as the dance requireth, for sometime there is made but 1 double and sometime 3 or 5 one after another and therefore is ddddd. thus written. And when r. is written, it betokeneth reprise, and if rrr. be written it signifieth 3 reprises, and rrrrr. betokeneth five. For ye ought never to make 2 nor 4 together, nor of the doubles also, for the doubles and the reprises are ever odd in number.

2.   Also all bace dances begin by singles or reverence and end with braule. Also it behoveth to know the number of notes of every bace dance, and the paces after the measure of the notes. Therefore ye ought to wit that first ye ought to make reverence with the left foot, and then a braule with the right foot, then two single paces, the first with the left foot and the second with the right foot in going forward, and ye must raise your body.

3.   The first double pace is made with the left foot in raising the body, stepping 3 paces forward lightly, the first with the left foot, the second with the right foot, and the third with the left foot, as the first.

4.   The second double pace beginneth with the right foot, going three paces forward as is said of the first in raising the body, etc.

5.   The third double pace is done as the first.

[1] Spelling modernized.

2

THE BASSE DANSE IN FRANCE

6. It is to note that there be never 2 double paces together, for the doubles and reprises be ever odd in number, 1, 3, or 5, etc.

7. A reprise alone ought to be made with the right foot in drawing the right foot backward a little to the other foot (i.e. *behind the other foot*).

8. The second reprise ought to be made (when ye make 3 at once) with the left foot in raising the body in like wise.

9. The third reprise is made in place [1] and as the first also.

10. And mark for all that is said that every (*one*) of these paces occupieth as much time the one as the other. That is to wit, a reverence, one note ; a double, one note ; two singles, one note ; a reprise, one note ; a braule, one note.

11. And ye ought to wit that in some places of France they call the reprises *desmarches*, and the braule they call *congé*, in English, leave.

This done, ye ought to put in writing for a reprise thus, r., and for three reprises thus, rrr., and for the braule thus, b.

BACE DANCES

Filles à marier, with IIII measures
    R. b. ss. ddd. rrr. b.
    ss. d. rrr. b.   Imperfect
    ss. ddd. ss. rrr. b.
    ss. d. ss. rrr. b.   Perfect

Le petit Rouen, with IIJI measures
    R. b. ss. ddddd. ss. rrr. b.
    ss. d. ss. rrr. b.
    ss. ddddd. ss. rrr. b   Perfect
    ss. ddd. ss. rrr. b.

Amours, with two measures
    R. b. ss. d. ss. rrr. b.
    ss. ddd. ss. rrr. b.   Perfect

La Gorrière, three measures
    R. b. ss. ddd. rrr. b.
    ss. d. r. b.   Imperfect
    ss. ddd. rrr. b.

[1] Turning obliquely towards the lady.

3

DANCES OF ENGLAND AND FRANCE

La allemande, three measures
    R. b. ss. ddd. ss. rrr. b.
    ss. d. ss. r. b.   Perfect
    ss. ddd. r. b.   Imperfect

La brette, four measures
    R. b. ss. d. ss. r. b.
    ss. d. r. b.
    ss. ddd. r. b.   Half perfect
    ss. d. ss. r. b.

La royne, four measures
    R. b. ss. ddd. r. b.
    ss. d. r. b.   Imperfect
    ss. ddd. r. b.
    ss. d. ss. r. b.   Perfect

These dances have I set at the end of this book to the intent that every learner of the said book after their diligent study may rejoice somewhat their spirits honestly in eschewing of idleness the portress of vices.

It will be noted that the above directions, though succinct in the main, leave certain important details unexplained. On the subject of the Reverence they are scanty; and the description of the branle step has been entirely omitted. The question of style, moreover, is barely hinted at; but these deficiencies are made good by other writers. The directions for the reprise, albeit lacking in detail, establish the point that in a sequence of reprises the movements, though performed with alternate feet, are yet identical in form. The meaning of the term " measure " as applied to the sections of a basse danse, and classified as " perfect " or " imperfect " is also made abundantly clear.

Of the seven dances set out at the conclusion of this little treatise, the first two, " Filles à marier " and " Le petit Rouen ", had evidently already enjoyed over a century of popularity, since we find them (fortunately accompanied by their appropriate music) in the *Livre de Basses danses de la Bibliothèque de Bourgogne* (*c.* 1450), and repeated in *Lart et Instruction de bien Dancer*, printed by Michel Toulouze (*c.* 1486). The scribe in the former work has omitted to put the musical clef in the case of " Filles à marier "; but happily this has been supplied by Michel Toulouze. This dance can therefore be included among the performing examples in the next chapter.

Let us now turn to the theoretical section of the *Livre de Basses danses de la Bibliothèque de Bourgogne*.

4

THE BASSE DANSE IN FRANCE

Monsieur Ernest Closson, who produced in 1912 a facsimile of this beautiful book (for the Société des Bibliophiles et Iconophiles de Belgique) informs us in his introductory commentary that the original order of the pages has been altered, since 1829, in which year Monsieur de Reiffenberg published an article on the manuscript which contained a complete transcription of the text. This important discovery enables me to quote the technical instructions in their correct order with a consequent gain in clarity.

1. *For the art and instruction of basse danse it should be noted that the basse danse primarily is divided into three parts. Namely into grand measure, into medium measure, and into little measure. The grand measure for entry of the basse danse should be trodden with one démarche. Then with a branle, then with two single paces, then with five double paces, then with two single paces, as before, then three démarches, then you must do a branle.*

2. *The medium measure should be trodden with two single paces, then with three double paces, then with two single paces, then three démarches, then you must do a branle.*

3. *The little measure should be trodden with two single paces, then with one double pace, then two single paces, then three démarches, and then a branle.*

4. *And it should be known that two single paces, one double pace, one démarche, and one branle occupy as much time the one as the other.*

5. *Item it should be noted that there are two manners of basse danse. That is to say basse danse mineur and basse danse majeur. Basse danse majeur begins as a basse danse, and for the first note which is named démarche, one makes a reverence to the lady, making an inclination towards her, and this inclination should be made with the left foot.*

6. *Basse danse mineur begins with the pas de Brabant, and with the first note of the basse danse one does not make a reverence to the lady.*

7. *It should be said that each one of them should occupy one basse danse note entire, that is to say two singles one note, a double pace one note, a démarche also one note, and likewise a branle.*

8. *And in these things is the basse danse correct and right in every detail.*

9. *Note that every basse danse begins by a démarche and finishes by a branle, and is named basse danse because it is played according to the major perfect (manner); and because, when one dances it, one goes serenely without extravagance of gesture, as gracefully as possible.*

10. *It should be known that there are never but two single paces together according to the art of good dancing.*

11. *Item it should be known that the double paces are always odd in number according to the art of good dancing truly.*

12. *Note that when one makes two single paces after the double pace one should make the first with the right foot, and the second with the left, so that one may make the first démarche with the right foot as is said above.*

B
5

13. *Item there is a general rule in basses danses that to begin with one makes a démarche, then one must make a branle and then two single paces, and then the double paces, and then two single paces if the measure of the basse danse requires it, and then the démarches and then the branle.*

14. *Item it should be noted that sometimes one makes one démarche and sometimes three.*

15. *Item it should be noted that there are some measures of the basses danses which are very perfect, the others are more than perfect, and the others are perfect, and the others imperfect.*

16. *The very perfect measures are those which have single paces before the double paces and (also) after, with three démarches and a branle.*

17. *The others are said to be perfect and are those which have single paces before the double paces, and after, with one démarche and one branle.*

18. *The others are called imperfect which have single paces before the double paces and not after, with three démarches and a branle.*

19. *Item in order to dance correctly a basse danse two things are required, firstly that one should know the number of steps of each basse danse, secondly that one should know how to make them go according to the number of the steps ; each basse danse will demonstrate this for you, since the number of steps has been devised for each basse danse ; it must be and thus is necessary to demonstrate and teach the manner in which one should perform the said steps.*

And firstly

20. *A single démarche (reprise) should be made with the right foot in retreating and is called démarche because one retreats, and should be made in raising of the body, and drawing back the right foot near to the other foot.*

21. *The second démarche should be made with the left foot in raising of the body and turning a little away from the lady and then bringing the right foot near to the left in raising of the body likewise.*

22. *The third should be made with the right foot as the first and should be made in the said place where was made the first (turning obliquely towards the lady).*

23. *The branle should begin with the left foot and should finish with the right foot, and is called branle because one makes it by swaying from one foot to the other.*

24. *The two single paces are made in advancing and the first single pace is made with the left foot in raising of the body and making one step forward, and the second single pace is made with the right foot and one should raise the body and advance a short distance.*

25. *The first double pace is made with the left foot and one should raise one's body and make three steps forward lightly. The first with the left foot, the second with the right, and the third with the left, like the first. The second double pace should be made with the right foot, and one should in like manner raise one's body and then make three steps forward,*

6

the first with the right foot, the second with the left, and the third with the right. The third double pace should be made with the left foot, like the first : the fourth is made with the right foot, like the second : the fifth is made with the left foot, like the first and like the third.

This treatise, whose style is somewhat prolix and at times involved, yet throws light on several points that are not touched on by Coplande. I have numbered its paragraphs in order to facilitate our comparison.

Paragraph 1 deals with three types of measure, used in the basse danse—the *Grand Measure*, proper to the Entry, the *Medium Measure*, and the *Little Measure*. This would appear to be the earliest classification of the measures, since in paragraphs 15–18 the subject of the measures is treated of anew ; and this time they are classified as *perfect*, in varying degrees, and *imperfect*. The perfection or imperfection depends upon whether the double paces are followed by a second pair of single paces, in which case the measure is *perfect*, or are immediately followed by the reprises and branle, this sequence rendering the measure *imperfect*. The various degrees of perfection, i.e. *very perfect*, *perfect*, and *more than perfect*, depend upon the number of consecutive double paces and reprises grouped in one measure. All of these varieties of perfection are, in Coplande's treatise, classified under one heading, as *perfect* ; while his *imperfect* measure corresponds with that demonstrated in the *Livre de Basses danses*.

To return to the older classification set forth in paragraph 1, the *Grand Measure*, suitable for the entry of the basse danse may be seen in Coplande's version of " Le petit Rouen ", used as the opening measure ; while the *Little Measure* forms the second section of this dance ; the latter half consists of the *Grand Measure* (without the reverence), followed by the *Medium Measure*.

This basse danse appears to be one of the earliest examples that have been preserved, and thus belongs to a time before the extreme popularity of the basse danse had caused almost any popular song to be pressed into its service, thereby introducing irregularity into the measures.

Its near contemporary, " Filles à marier," has its first two measures *imperfect*, which measures can also be classed as *medium* and *little*, under the older classification ; while the second half of this dance, which is *perfect*, consists likewise of the *Medium* and *Little* Measures.

The purpose of these classifications would seem to be primarily for the guidance of the Masters, who devised the dances, and secondly, to help the memory of the dancers ; since the branle step, which terminates each measure, does not necessarily coincide with a halting place in the music, except in the case of the finale, wherein the last branle is crowned by a parting reverence termed *congé*.

The text of paragraph 4 informs us that all the steps of the basse danse occupy as much time, the one as the other, which information is reiterated in paragraph 7, with the difference that it is said that each step occupies one note of the basse danse.

Paragraphs 5 and 6 speak of two manners of basse danse, namely, Major and Minor, the one being a true basse danse throughout, whereas the other is a light movement of the Saltarello type used in conjunction with the basse danse by way of contrast, and termed variously the " Schiolta ", " Gioiosa ", " Alta ", " Saltarello ", " Recoupe ", etc. This light movement dispensed with the formal reverence ; and its steps, known as the " pas de Brabant ", were lightened by hops. These will be explained later.

Paragraph 8 appears to close the subject, declaring that in these things is the basse danse correct and right in every detail.

Paragraph 9 describes the *style* proper to the basse danse, emphasizing its gracious serenity.

The succeeding paragraphs are concerned with minor points, until we arrive at numbers 15 to 18, which treat of the second classification of the measures already alluded to.

Number 19 is a preamble to the last section consisting of numbers 20–25, which explain the steps in detail, including important points connected with the reprise, herein called the *démarche* (although noted with an r. in the step tablature) ; and concludes with the branle. When one realizes that, whereas the single and double paces are performed fronting the onlookers and advancing, the reprise and *branle* are done facing obliquely sideways (the reprise in retreat and the *branle* stationary), these directions become easily intelligible.

I would here mention that all the treatises describe the steps as they are executed by the *man* ; and that, since it is necessary that the partners should face one another for the *démarche*, the *branle*, and the final *congé*, the lady must throughout use the opposite foot from that of the man.

Earlier in this chapter reference was made to a work of unknown authorship entitled *Lart et Instruction de bien Danser*, printed in Paris (*c.* 1486) by Michel Toulouze. This little book, of which the only known copy was discovered in recent years in the library of the Royal College of Physicians, was reprinted in facsimile in 1936 by Emery Walker, Ltd., at the request of the College. The reprint also contains a bibliographical introduction by Victor Scholderer. This treatise amounts to an abridged version of the *Livre de Basses danses de Bourgogne*, with certain small differences. In the description of the *démarche* or reprise, and also of the first single pace, an *inclination* of the body is enjoined in place of the *raising* thereof. In performance we find that the so-called " raising of the body ", which means rising on the toe with straightened knee, is usually preceded by a *lowering* of the body, accomplished by bending the knee of the stationary leg on which the weight of the body rests. The rising takes place in the latter half of the step, thus producing the undulating movement alluded to by the Italian Masters.

Of the forty-eight dances given with the appropriate music at the close of the technical explanations in *Lart et Instruction de bien Danser*, forty-one are to be found in the *Livre de Basses danses de Bourgogne*. The music printing is rough in comparison with the exquisitely refined penmanship of this superb manuscript. One of the dances reproduced from the *Livre de Basses danses* has a different tune (" Le grant Thozin ").

We now arrive at a feature of primary importance. All these treatises stress the point that every complete step of the basse danse occupies as much time the one as the other, this time measure being *one note of the basse danse*. In this connection the word *note* does not refer to a musical note but to a measure of four beats at a slow tempo. For enlightenment on this point we can turn to the treatises of Antonius de Arena and Thoinot Arbeau (1536 and 1588 respectively).

Arena's versified treatise contains a postscript in prose which states that all common (regular) basses danses are danced to twenty longs, and that each long is composed of four semibreves. He then gives the established sequence of steps of a *regular* basse danse, which steps are twenty in number, making eighty semibreves in all. (Note the disappearance of the measures.) He refers us back to the couplets describing the steps. In these, despite the stilted style, due to the artificial medium, we can glean some helpful information on the Provençal manner of performing the basse danse in the late fifteenth and early sixteenth centuries. The couplet, beginning : " Passibus ergo duplum de tribus esse memento," informs us in involved language that the double pace is made out of three steps, of which one is retarded. The feet in walking, however, mark *four* beats. Of these, the first two are made by one foot, the third by the other foot, and the fourth by the first one. The meaning of this (as we learn from other sources) is that on the first beat the dancer marks time with his toe beside the stationary foot and on the second beat he makes his first step. On the third beat the reverse foot steps and on the fourth beat the first foot again, thus completing the composite movement, known as a *double pace*.

The same procedure applies to the single paces, the step being made on the off beat. Arbeau says in this connection : *Arena and others of his following make the single with one and the same foot, marking the first beat with the left foot beside the right, and then advancing the said left. And the same with the right foot : but I remember that my master in Poitiers disapproved of this mode, saying that it was more seemly to finish the two singles with the feet joined together* (first position, in modern dancing) *than by the advancing of one of the feet.* By this innovation of stepping on the accented beat and the bringing forward of the other foot, in line with the first, on the off beat, Arbeau robs the basse danse of something of its fluent medieval grace, approaching it to the weightiness of the pavan.

Mention is made both by Arena and Arbeau of the occasional performance of the basse danse by three dancers, the man being in the centre with a lady on either hand ; but this practice is discouraged by both writers on account of the complications introduced in the interchange of courtesies.

To his rules for the single paces Arena adds an injunction, reiterated by Arbeau, to beware of making the steps too large, as though establishing a measurement, adding that *Bartholus* teaches that the steps in the basse danse should be small.

Next we come to the *reprise*. Here we find that this step, as used in Provence at this period, is not of the kind that we have hitherto seen described in connection with the basse danse (the which corresponds to the Italian *Reprisa Grave*), but is the *Reprisa Minuita*. This step is excellently explained by Cesare Negri as follows :—

Translation.

The Diminished Reprise

The diminished reprise of the ladies is done in this manner, standing with the feet equal and the heels as near together as one finger's breadth, and the points separated by four (fingers' breadth) from each other ; then join both the points of the feet together, and, widening the space between the heels, you will once again join the heels and separate the points, and this you will do four times, progressing towards the left with great rapidity. I warn you that you should stand with the whole body erect, keeping the feet flat upon the ground and making no movement save with the feet only and thus you will make a beautiful and graceful appearance : this reprise has taken the name of minuita.

La Ripresa Minuita [1] (original wording)

" La ripresa minuita delle dame si fa in questo modo stando con amendue i piè pari con le calcagna appresso un dito & le punte de' piedi discoste quattro l'uno dall'altro : poi si giungeranno tutte due le punte de i piedi al pari, & allargando altretanto le calcagna si farà'l medisimo giungendo esse calcagna, & allargando le punte, & questo si faranno quattro volte alla sinistra con prestezza, avertendo che s'hà da stare con la persona dritta, tenendo bene spianati i piedi in terra, & non muoverà altro che li piedi soli & così farà bella, e gratiosa vista : questa ripresa con li piedi pari ha preso questo nome di minuita."

This ornate step is still used in peasant dances of Eastern Europe. The period of Cesare Negri is not so far removed from that of Arena as would appear, because Cesare Negri informs us that he established his school of dancing in Milan in 1554 ; at which date he would have been about twenty years old.

Arena's mode of describing the diminished reprise, which is more obscure than that of Negri, I would translate as follows : *Now comes the reprise ; but it is not performed advancing, but sideways ; for it is ornamented in the intricate manner*

[1] Nuove Inventioni di Balli, Milan, 1604.

("nam tricotare decet"), *and gliding always towards the right, agitating the legs and moving the feet. In joining shoulders with the lady, take care not to bump against her in your rapid approach, for if you should jostle her too much, you might cause the maiden to stagger backwards. Because of such small occurrences a woman always scolds a lover. And, in doing this, retreat four beats. But let the detached foot at that time make contact with the other foot. Three beats one leg pulsates towards the right; the left leg will give one beat only. The first two beats does the right leg perform and then the other leg will give one. The fourth step, however, will be made in reverse by the leg which will have made the first two. And this you may accomplish by bodily vigour, but will easily know when you will be well skilled.*

Where, for the sake of the verse, the clarity of the explanation is sacrificed, I have tried to give the meaning of the phrases rather than the literal words. The statement that three beats are made with the right foot and one with the left sounds bewildering, but means in reality that for three beats the right leg controls the direction of the movement; because, in order that this may progress towards the right, the heel of the right foot must at the start separate from the left. When the movement is leftwards, it is the left heel that first separates; but in each case the feet are instantly reunited at the points. In the same vague manner Coplande speaks of the branle as being done with the *right foot;* and the author of the *Livre de Basses danses* says, when describing a sequence of five double paces, that the third should be done with the *left foot*, like the first, the fourth with the *right foot*, etc. The supposed risk of a collision between the partners arises from the fact that they perform their retreat at an oblique angle, tending to come together at the close of the second and fourth beats.

The succeeding stanza Arena devotes to the *branle step*, termed by him "congedium". With regard to this unusual nomenclature, Arbeau writes as follows in *Orchésographie : The branle is called by Arena " Congedium " and I think that he means it thus because, from the appearance of the dancer's gesture, it would seem that he was about to finish and take leave (" prendre congé "); and nevertheless, after the branle he continues his steps and movements. . . .*

The term *congé* is normally applied by all writers, including Arena, to the leave-taking at the close of the basse danse. In truth the branle step is of the nature of a salutation, though not accompanied by the bending of the knee and drawing back of one foot. On this subject Arena says : *In the Congé (branle) one dances only with the body, swaying the body, not moving the feet. But when, on the contrary, you draw back the left leg in courtly fashion (" amice "), the right leg then governs the whole person. In dances of intermediate character (" in medio dansae ") you never make the congé (branle) unless the reprise be duly joined to it. But you will often see the reprise without the congé in Basses danses, if so be that you dance them. But such do not serve our gay times; all dancers nowadays want to dance in sprightly fashion. . .*

DANCES OF ENGLAND AND FRANCE

Arbeau agrees with Arena in classing the basse danse as intermediate between the solemn pavan and the more lively dances and when describing the passomezzo (a quicker pavan with ornamented steps), he says that it is of lighter measure than the pavan, " et par ce moyen elle se ressente de la médiocrité d'une basse dance " (Arbeau writes the name thus with a " c ").

Arena's description of the opening salutation termed *Reverenza* agrees with that of the earlier writers including the drawing back of the left leg. For this he uses the word " fauchare ", which implies that the leg moves in semi-circular fashion like a scythe. The lady is directed to curtsey by bending the knees and keeping the feet joined. Arena's treatise is enlivened throughout by a spirit of gay humour. In urging on all young men the manifold advantages of cultivating the art of dancing, he tells them that in heaven the angels dance their rounds to the sound of the organ.

Let us now consider the final modifications in the French basse danse recorded by Arbeau with admirable care.[1] Speaking of the dances most in favour in the preceding generation (" du temps de nos pères "), he mentions " pavanes, basses dances, branles, et courantes ", adding, " les basses dances sont hors d'usage depuis quarante ou cinquante ans." The dances of those times, he says, were commonly accompanied by the pipe and tabour, so that a single musician sufficed to play both, *and make the symphony and accordance complete.*

His pupil Capriol asks : *How did our fathers dance the basse danse?* Arbeau replies : *They had two kinds of basses danses, the one common and regular, the other irregular. The regular ones were appropriate to those songs that were regular, and the irregular ones to the irregular songs.*

Capriol : *What do you call common and regular?*

Arbeau : *The musicians of that time composed their songs in sixteen bars (" mesures ") which they repeated, and thus there were thirty-two bars for the beginning; and for the middle section they put sixteen bars, and for the end, sixteen bars repeated, which made thirty-two bars. Thus in all there were eighty bars, of which the common and regular basse danse is composed.[2] And if by chance the tune of the song went beyond these eighty bars, the basse danse played on this one was called irregular. . . .*

Capriol : *What movements were to be done during these bars?*

Arbeau : *First you must know that the songs of the basse danse are played in triple time, and in each bar the tabour, to be in accordance with the flute, makes also triple time, in beating these said eighty bars with its little stick; the said bars consisting of a minim and four crotchets thus : —*

---

[1] *Orchésographie* written in the form of a dialogue, published 1588.
[2] This corresponds with Arena's eighty semibreves.

and to each bar the dancer makes the movements of feet and body according to the precepts of the dance. Asked by Capriol in what these movements of the dance consist, Arbeau replies : *The first movement is the reverence, marked with a capital R., the second sort of movement is the branle, marked by a b. The third sort of movement is the two singles, marked by SS. The fourth sort of movement is the reprise marked by a small r.*

Hereupon arises an interesting point, for on Capriol's asking whether these are all the movements in the basse danse, Arbeau says : *There are no other kinds of movements in the said basse danse, nor in the return of the basse danse ("ny au retour de la basse dance"), although the said kinds are repeated several times.* Interrogated as to the meaning of this expression " the return of the basse danse ", Arbeau replies : *The basse dance in its entirety contains three parts : the first part is called " basse dance " ; the second part is called " retour de la basse dance " ; and the third and last part is called " tordion ".* . . . . He proceeds to reproduce the step tablature of a regular basse danse of twenty longs exactly as it stands in Arena's prose sequel to his treatise. He then reproduces a second section of step tablature conforming to twelve longs, as given by Arena under the heading of " La moitié à XII ". Arbeau terms this section the *return of the vasse dance* (thus interpreting " La moitié ") for which the dancers are directed to pass round the room conversing in courtly fashion until they reach their starting point whence they perform an extra section of the basse danse containing twelve steps. In reality this " moitié " is another name for the light movement which sometimes followed the basse danse and is designated in the *Livre de Basses danses* as " Basse danse Mineur ", whose steps are hopped and performed to a lighter rhythm in triple time. The ancient " basse danse Majeur " was always in duple time, but by the sixteenth century there were some examples to be met with in triple time ; and, contrary to Arbeau's impression, several of these occur among the publications of Pierre Attaignant dating 1529. The light movement is named by him " recoupe ". These ornate or *cut* steps were called by the earlier writers " pas de Brabant ", and form the basic steps of the Saltarello. It was considered that by the lightening of the steps with hops or flourishes they were thereby divided or halved. This cutting of the steps is alluded to by Arbeau when he describes the Spanish Pavan where he says " laquelle se danse découpée avec diversité de gestes ".

Arena, in his inventory of fifty-nine irregular basses danses with their tablature, makes no further mention of this " moitié à XII " ; but among the basses danses published by Pierre Attaignant several have their light movement and some also a tordion. One of these will be included among our performing examples.

It now remains for us to pass in survey the modifications which Arbeau introduces into the basse danse steps, in their order. He says : *The Reverence, first gesture and movement, holds four batteries of the drum which accompany four bars of the song played by the flute. Anthoine Arena, considering that all dances begin with the left foot, was of opinion that the reverence should be made with the left foot ; however, it seems in the end that he leaves it doubtful, saying thus :*

    Bragardi certant & adhuc sub judice lis est
    De quali gamba sit facienda salus.

As to me I am of the opinion of my master under whom I studied in former times in Pottiers that one should make it with the right foot : thus doing, one is able to turn the body and the face towards the damsel and cast upon her a gracious look.

2. The branle : *The said branle is made in four drum batteries which accompany four bars of the song played by the flute, keeping the feet joined, swaying the body gently towards the left for the first bar, then towards the right, regarding the assembly modestly, for the second bar, then again towards the left for the third bar ; and for the fourth bar towards the right, regarding the damsel with a respectful glance, gently and discreetly* (" d'une oeillade desrobée doulcement et discretement ").

3. The singles : *You will walk forward with the left foot for the first bar : Then join the right foot to the said left for the second bar : Then you will advance the right foot for the third bar : And at the fourth bar and beat you will join the left foot with the said right foot, and thus will be perfect the movement of the two singles : And you must beware of making the paces so large that it seems as though one intended to measure the length of the hall, besides which the lady could scarcely with modesty take such long steps as you yourself would make.*

4. The doubles : These are described by Arbeau after the same system as the singles, i.e. stepping on the first beat and concluding on the fourth by joining the feet in the first position. I doubt that the singles and doubles of the *basse danse* were ever performed thus.

5. The reprise : Capriol inquires how the reprise is made and is told : *The movement called reprise precedes ordinarily the branle and sometimes the double and holds four bars of the drum the same as the other movements, the which you will do in moving a little the knees, or the feet, or the toes only, as though your feet shivered. Namely on the first bar the toes of the right foot, then again the said toes of the right foot on the second bar, then the toes of the left foot on the third bar, and the toes of the said right foot on the fourth bar : And in these four movements is the reprise accomplished, and the dancer ready to do the branle or the other movements which follow.*

It is this passage which convinces me that Arbeau had never seen the basse danse performed, but is merely trying to interpret Arena's more than ordinarily obscure directions. Whenever Arbeau is describing a dance that he has himself danced, his directions are remarkably lucid ; but with regard to the above, I have never yet met a person able to perform the diminished reprise, unaided by any explanations other than these.

Capriol, however, appears satisfied, and next discusses the subject of the four beats or bars allotted to every complete basse danse step, saying : *If we would call the four bars of the drum and the flute a quaternion or tetradon : I find, counting the characters which you have given me, from memory, that the basse danse contains twenty quaternions : and the return of the basse danse contains twelve quaternions.*

Arbeau : *The suggestion is good : and after the basse danse and the return of the basse danse you will be able to begin the tourdion. . . .* The name quaternion is useful to indicate the time measure of a basse danse step, amounting as it does to one *long*, divided into four beats of one semibreve each. In Arbeau's arrangement of " Jouissance vous donneray ", the four semibreves are thereby converted into four *dotted* semibreves, which does not affect the time measure, as Arbeau points out. After telling Capriol that he can find a good number of pavans and basses danses in the dance books of Pierre Attaignant and the late Master Nicholas, he says : *In any case you will have to turn into triple time the said basses danses, the which are set in duple time.* Capriol suggests that Arbeau should do this for him, writing them down ; but Arbeau replies : *When one knows the steps and movements of one pavan and one basse danse, one can dance all the others : for although they are of different tunes and they are sung and played in diverse manners, they are alike in measure* (time measure).

While the appropriate drum beat for the " mesure ternaire " has been shown by Arbeau as one minim and *four* crotchets, that for " mesure binaire " is given as one minim and *two* crotchets. By way of illustration I give the first quaternion of " Jouissance vous donneray ", as reduced by Arbeau to *mesure ternaire*, and the same in a version of this song arranged in florid style for keyboard in Attaignant's publication, *Vingt et six chansons musicales reduictes en la tablature des Orgues, Espinettes Manicordions & telz semblables instruments musicaulx* (Paris, 1530).

The tune is herein given in G minor, but to facilitate comparison I will here transpose it into D minor as has been done by Arbeau, giving only the line of the melody with appropriate drum battery for duple time.

JOUISSANCE.

This much ornamented version is not presented by Attaignant as a basse danse but as a setting of the song in the ornate style appropriate to the keyboard music of this period.

Concerning the use of the drum, Capriol asks : *Is it necessary that in pavans and basses danses the tabour and flute should be employed?* Arbeau replies : *Not unless one wishes : for one can play them on violins, spinets, transverse flutes, recorders, oboes, and all kinds of instruments, such as singing them with voices : but the tabour helps marvellously with its uniform beat in the posing of the feet according to the correct proportion of the movements.*

The time value apportioned to each of these beats by Arena was noted as a semibreve. Nowadays in accordance with the tendency of notational values to go on doubling themselves, we should feel inclined to note these beats in minims, whereas in the century preceding Arena's dancing days they would have been noted in breves and earlier still, when the basse danse was at the outset of its career, possibly in longs. However, it is not the written value that is of importance but the slow rhythmic pulsations which the dancer cannot help but feel. For, just as there is a limit to the speed of successive pulsations to which the body can respond, so also is there a limit to the slowness ; and one who has performed a number of basses danses becomes readily sensitive to the correct tempo. Noting therefore our four beats in semibreves according to the system of Arena, I would fix the tempo at o = 48 on the metronome.

Arbeau's remark as to the helpfulness of the drum beats is certainly true where the music contains syncopations as in the following example :

Basse danse à 5 Parties.   *Pierre Attaignant 1529.*

This example forms part of a collection of basses danses, pavans, and

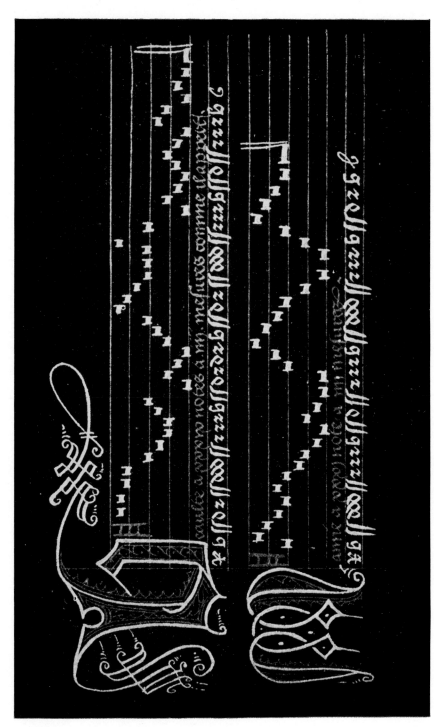

Facsimile of a page from *Livre de Basses danses de Marie de Bourgogne*
(inscribed in gold and silver on a black ground).

Bibliothèque Royale de Belgique.

[face p. 16

galliards, set for stringed or wind instruments, published by Pierre Attaignant in 1529, under the title *Dixhuit basses danses*.

The *Livre de Basses danses de Bourgogne* appears to have been compiled from more than one previous treatise, the most ancient part being contained in paragraphs 1 to 8. The tunes likewise are of various periods as is clear from the character of the music. The pattern of the measures has become irregular in some of the later dances, thereby making them difficult to memorize.

One of the apparently most ancient dances in this collection is " Filles à marier ". It would seem to have attained a wide popularity, since we meet with it, not only in the treatises of Michel Toulouze and Coplande, but also in a surviving fragment of a Catalan dance-book of the fifteenth century,[1] discovered by Señor Aurelio Capmany, hidden among the municipal Archives of Cervera in Castile, and reproduced in his book *El Baile y la Danza* (1931). The tune is of the kind described once by Arnold Dolmetsch as being one of those " *fundamental . . . eternal tunes which one never feels tired of hearing* ".

[1] In this book the name of the dance has been transformed into " Filles à Maria ".

The speech of Love :—

Stanza 46　*And thou, sweet music, dancing's only life,*
The ear's sole happiness, the air's best speech,
Lodestone of fellowship, charming-rod of strife,
The soft mind's paradise, the sick mind's leech,
With thine own tongue thou trees and stones canst teach,
That when the air doth dance her finest measure,
Then art thou born, the gods' and men's sweet pleasure.

*　*　*　*

Concord.

Stanza 109　The richest jewel in all the heavenly treasure
That ever yet unto the earth was shown
Is perfect concord, th' only perfect pleasure
That wretched earth-born men have ever known ;
For many hearts it doth compound in one,
That whatso one doth will or speak or do
With one consent they all agree thereto.

(Orchestra)

CHAPTER II

HOW TO DANCE THE BASSE DANSE

IN the basse danse the couple stands side by side holding hands, with the lady's hand held uppermost and raised to about the level of her shoulder. She stands on the man's right, giving him her left hand.

The dance consists of advances and retreats punctuated by the stationary step called " branle ". The advancing movements exceed the retreats so that a gradual progress is made up the centre line towards the onlookers. When the head of the dance is reached, the couple can either effect a gradual receding movement by making the alternate double paces backwards or else, making a quarter turn, describe a circular movement or a looping pattern, provided that they finish on the central line in order to make their parting salutation to the assembled company. The steps should be *very small*.

The Positions

1st	♭♩	Position			
2nd	♭ ♩	Position			
3rd	♭♩	right		♩♭	left
4th	♭ ♩	right		♭ ♩	left
5th	♭ ♩	right		♭ ♩	left

The Steps

They are the Reverence : R.
           the Branle : b.
           the Two Singles : SS.
           the Double : d.
           the Reprise : r.

The Reverence : To perform the reverence the partners should face each other, not directly, but making an oblique angle like the letter V.

The Man : On the first beat the man stands still with the left foot forward in the fourth position (described as fourth position, left) ; on the second beat he draws it back with a semicircular motion till the toe rests a few inches behind the heel of the right foot. During this time the weight of the body rests on the right foot and in drawing back the left foot the dancer inclines his head and body ; on the third beat he bends both knees outwards and transfers his weight backwards on to the left foot, straightening the right knee ; on the fourth beat, returning the weight forward on to the right foot and rising on the toes, he joins the left foot up behind the right in the third position (called the third position, right), and sinks on to the flat of the feet at the close.

The Lady : The lady should keep her feet joined in the third position left. On the first beat she stands still ; on the second beat she rises a little on the toes ; on the third beat she sinks, bending both knees outwards ; on the third *half* beat she rises once more a little on the toes, and on the fourth beat she descends on to the flat of the feet.

Arm Movements : If the man is wearing a hat, he should on the first beat raise his left hand and grasp the brim between fingers and thumb ; on the second beat, he removes it with a downward and outward sweep of the arm, keeping the inside of the hat turned towards his left side ; on the third beat he raises the hat towards his head, and on the fourth plants it firmly in place. Should he dance without a hat, he can make moderate gestures, drawing the hand inward and upward for the first and second beats, and lowering it outward in a graceful curve for the third and fourth beats. The lady makes the same gestures with her free hand.

The Branle : Turned towards one another obliquely, with feet in the third position and inside foot in front (man right, lady left), the dancers, on the first beat, sway the body outwards, putting the weight on the outer foot and lifting the heel of the inside foot. The second beat is marked by a graceful inclination of the head. For the third and fourth beats they reverse the movement, swaying towards the inner side and transferring the weight to the inside foot. The transferring of the weight from side to side enhances the grace of the branle step. Arbeau, in his explanation of this step, doubles the movement, making the dancers sway outwards and inwards twice during the four beats, in which manner the gesture would be less profound. The older writers imply that it is done only once each way during the four beats.

Singles : First beat ; bend the knees outwards, marking time with the toe of the moving foot against the heel of the stationary foot. Second beat ; step and rise on toes with straightened knees. Third and fourth beats ; repeat the step in like manner with the reverse foot. The first pair of singles begins with the outside foot (man left, woman right), but, where the ensuing double or doubles are followed by another pair of singles, it starts perforce with the inside foot.

Doubles : The double consists of three steps. First beat : bend the knees outwards, marking time with the moving foot against the heel of the stationary foot. Second beat : step and rise on toes. Third beat : bend knee of first foot slightly and step with reverse foot, but in posing the foot, rise instantly on the toes. Fourth beat : step with first foot with straightened leg, landing on the toe, but sinking again on to the flat of the foot. The first double starts with the outside foot (man left, woman right), the second with the inside foot, and the third with the outside foot, like the first. With practice the movements melt into one another, producing the undulating effect characteristic of the basse danse. The steps should be small and performed in a gliding manner. In the second step of the double (third beat) the bending should anticipate the beat.

The Reprise : Make an eighth turn inwards on the toe of the outside foot, so as to face towards partner at an oblique angle. On the first beat bend the knee of the outside leg and, with the inside foot, step sideways in retreat : on the second beat rise on the toes of both feet : on the third beat join up the outside foot, placing it behind the other in the third position : on the fourth beat, make a quarter turn outwards on the toes, turning away from partner, and landing on the flat of the feet in the third position *reversed*—that is, with the man's right foot behind the heel of his left foot and the lady's left foot behind her right.

Second Reprise : The partners, being now turned away from one another slightly, make, on the first beat, a sideways step in retreat with reverse feet (the man with his left and the woman with her right), and proceed as with the first *reprise.* On the fourth beat they make the quarter-turn inwards, landing in the third position as before, the man with his right foot in front and the woman with her left. The third *reprise* is made like the first except that on the fourth beat, instead of making a quarter-turn outwards (as in the first), the dancers remain facing one another at an oblique angle, merely sinking to the flat of the front foot, on which the weight should rest preparatory to performing the branle which closes each measure. In the case of the later, unsystematic basses danses, of which there are some examples in the *Livre de Basses danses de la Bibliothèque de Bourgogne,* wherein a *reprise* may be followed by a double, the dancers would need to make an eighth of a turn outwards so as to face the spectators for the renewed advance. Likewise after each branle that terminates the successive measures, the dancers must make this eighth of a turn outwards so as to face forward for the ensuing pair of singles.

At the close of the dance the partners make their reverence, called *congé,* towards each other, before advancing to salute the assembly. During the branle step the free arm should be bent at the elbow and the palm of the hand turned upwards for the outward swaying and downwards for the inward movement.

When making the pair of single paces, the dancer will find that a semi-circular arm movement inwards, from the elbow, during the first and second beats and outwards during the third and fourth, balances the movement of the feet. The same accords well with the doubles and *reprises.* These gestures should be done gently and easily.

The following dances (set for the keyboard and with their steps clearly allocated) have been selected from the *Livre de Basses danses de la Bibliothèque de Bourgogne*, as representative of the various types of basse danse contained in this collection. The first two appear to be the most ancient; the third, " Beaulté," is of an intermediate type, and the fourth, " La Franchoise Nouvelle," which is the last basse danse in the book, is of later date, its music being given in sixteenth-century notation with bar lines. At the close of this tune there occurs a bar line followed by repeat marks, then double bar lines followed again by repeat marks. These indications are supplemented by directions that it is to be played twice, which I interpreted as meaning twice with repeats. This proved to be correct, as, so performed, the music contains the requisite number of quaternions to accord with the steps indicated. " La Franchoise Nouvelle " occupies one entire page and is complete in itself. The lines of music which follow it in the manuscript are merely the continuation of " La Danse de Cleves ", which dance begins on the preceding page. This is a dance of a Balletto type, containing evolutions in which the couple separate and reunite. I conclude therefore that " La Franchoise Nouvelle " should have preceded " La Danse de Cleves ", but that the leaf had been accidentally turned round during repairs so that the *recto* becomes the *verso*.

BASSE DANSE " FILLES A MARIER "

Set by Mabel Dolmetsch.   *Bibliothèque de Bourgogne.*

R.b.SS.d.d.d.SS.r.r.r.b.SS.d.r.r.r.b.

SS.d.d.d.SS.r.r.r.b.SS.d.r.r.r.b.

(Steps from Michel Toulouze)

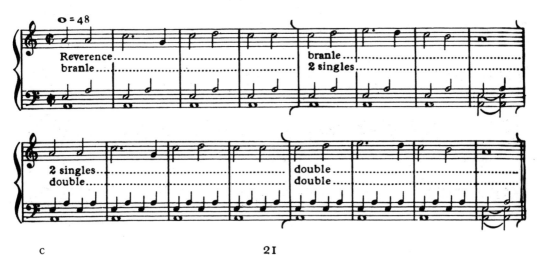

DANCES OF ENGLAND AND FRANCE

HOW TO DANCE THE BASSE DANSE

LE PETIT ROUEN

Set by Mabel Dolmetsch.   Bibliothèque de Bourgogne.

R.b.SS.ddddd.SS.rrr.b.SS.d.SS.rrr.b.SS.ddddd.SS.rrr.b.
SS.ddd.SS.rrr.b.

The whole to be played
straight through four times

Da Capo

23

DANCES OF ENGLAND AND FRANCE

BASSE DANSE "BEAULTÉ"

Set by Arnold Dolmetsch.   *Bibliothèque de Bourgogne.*

R . b . SS . d . r . SS . d . d . d . SS . r . r . r . b . SS . d . r . d . r . b .

SS . d . r . SS . d . d . d . SS . r . r . r . b . SS . d . SS . r . r . r . b . C. Congé

24

HOW TO DANCE THE BASSE DANSE

(VARIATION by CARL DOLMETSCH)

congé

25

DANCES OF ENGLAND AND FRANCE

BASSE DANSE " LA FRANCHOISE NOUVELLE "

Set by Arnold Dolmetsch.   *Bibliothèque de Bourgogne.*

R.b.SS.d.d.d.SS.r.SS.d.r.b.
SS.d.d.d.r.d.r.b.SS.d.r.b. Congé

26

The next development of the basse danse, of which we have documentary evidence, is the Provençal variety, described by Antonius de Arena. From his extensive inventory of "Basses danses non communes" I have selected three, namely—"L'amour de moy", "Hélas Madame", and "Patience"; and to these I will add Arbeau's version of "Jouissance vous donneray", whose tune is most attractive. The first two tunes are contained in the *Manuscrit de*

Bayeux (fifteenth century), wherein they are given with all their words. The third, "Patience" (which is cited also by Arbeau), is one of a collection of dance tunes arranged for the lute, published by Pierre Attaignant (*Dixhuit basses danses*, Paris, 1529).

All of these dance tunes are here given, set for the keyboard as being the most convenient arrangement.

The steps should be performed in the same manner as in the older basse danse, with the exception of the *reprise*, which should be done as a "reprisa minuita" in the following manner : Facing your partner at an oblique angle so as to form a V, and standing with heels joined in the first position, make a retreat by moving sideways, first the heel of the inside foot and the toe of the outside foot (so that the heels become separated and the toes joined), then the toe of the inside foot and the heel of the outside foot (so that the heels are again joined and the toes separated in the first position). Do this double movement twice for the first beat and twice for the second beat, thereby executing a smooth gliding retreat. For the third beat go in the contrary direction towards the audience by moving first the heel of the outside foot and the toe of the inside foot, and then the toe of the outside foot and the heel of the inside foot. Do this double movement twice, coming to a halt in the first position at the close of the third beat. For the fourth beat retreat once more with the same movements as in the first two beats. This completes the *reprisa minuita*, which always occurs singly in the Provençal basse danse. These movements of heel and toe should be small and smoothly executed. As the dancers grow skilled the motion becomes rapid and one ceases to count the movements, as in a well performed trill. There must be no movement of head, body, or arms, and the dancers should stand with head erect.

BASSE DANSE "L'AMOUR DE MOY"
R.b.SS.d.SS.r.d.SS.r.b.SS.ddd.SS.r.d.SS.r.b. (2 measures)

HOW TO DANCE THE BASSE DANSE

29

DANCES OF ENGLAND AND FRANCE

Ce jar-din est bel - et plai-sant; il est gar-ni de tou - te fleur.

On y prend son é - bat-te - ment, Au - tant la

nuit com - me le jour. (Ritornelle)

Hé - las il est si dou - ce cho -

- se que de ce doux ros - sig-nol - let,

qui chante au soir au ma - - - ti - net; quand il est

las il se re - po - - se. Je la vis l'au -

- tre jour cueill - ir la Vi - ol - lette en un vert pré;

la plus bel - le qu'on ques je veis, et la plus plai - sante

à mon gré. (Ritornelle)

This song contains a final stanza, to be sung to the first section of the tune, which has not been allowed for in the dance as devised by Arena. If it is desired to include this, a third measure should be added as follows. SS.d.SS.r.b.

31

Je la re - gar - de u - ne po - - - se, Elle e-

-tait blan - che __ comme lait et dou-ce comme __ un a - gnol

-let, Ver - meil-let - te comme u - ne Ro - - - se.

BASSE DANSE "HÉLAS MADAME"
R.b.SS.d.(SS).r.b.SS.d.SS.r.b.SS.ddd.(SS).r.b.SS.d·SS.r.b.

To be played six times

VOICE PART

"Hé - las ma da - me que je dé - si - re tant, Souf-frez que soye __ vos-

-tre loy - al a - mant. Tout mon vi - vant, tou-jours vous ser-vi - rai.

HOW TO DANCE THE BASSE DANSE

Car vos-tre suis____ et tou-jours le se - rai. Tou-tes sont da - mes par

a-mour ce dit on. Mais n'y a peu____ qui en ay-ent le re - nom.

Et pour quoy non? Car trop voul-lez choi - sir. Pre - nez en

un ____ et lui fait - es plai - sir. Hé - las, beau si - re, vous

ê - tes bel et bon, Sage et cour-toys ____ et de no - ble mai - son

et aus-si bon que l'on saur-ait fi - ner, Mais cil que j'ay - me, ne

sau-rais ou-bli - er." "Hé - las, ma da - me, pen-sez en vot-re cas:

En - tre nous deux ____ ne faut point d'a - vo - cats." "Cer - tes non pas, et

vous le sav-ez bien. Al - lez vous en;____ car vous ne fai - tes rien."

"Mon cœur sous-pi - re et se plaint ten-dre-ment, quand il ne peut____ trou-

-ver al - lé - ge - ment. Ne sait com-ment on me veut dé-chas-ser;

Sil est ain - si____ j'i - rai ail-leurs chas-ser: Hé - las, ma da - me, et

n'en se-ray-je point?" "Cer-tes beau sire, — je ne le vous dis point. Ser-vez à

point: il vous se-ra me-ry." Hé-las, ma da - me, de bon cœur vous mer-cy."

Basse danse " Patience " is one of those to which a light movement (called in this instance *recoupe*) and a tordion [1] have been added. The steps of the recoupe are nominally of the same kind as those employed in the *Basse danse Majeur*, but they are " broken " or ornamented and lightened by hops. In the fifteenth century these broken steps were known as *pas de Brabant*, but in the late sixteenth century the Italian masters called them *spezzate*. I must here explain that the terms *single, double*, and *reprise* are names for fundamental movements that may be modified in various ways according to the type of dance to which they are adapted. For example, a single may be glided, trodden, or stepped in a challenging manner with uneven beats (in which case it is called a *puntata*). It may also be broken and hopped, and it can be danced forwards, backwards, or sideways. When done with a sideways spring with the other foot raised, it becomes a " trabuchetto ".

The *branle step* in the light movement can also be ornamented by doubling the movement, swaying outwards and inwards twice during the four bars, in the manner prescribed by Arbeau, in which case the inclinations are less profound.

The *reprise* was used as a retreat and as a change of direction (being also called *démarche* and *déroutement*) : it can take many forms. These are the *Reprisa grave* or *slow reprise*, as used in the early basses danses, the *Reprisa minima* or *lesser reprise*, the *Reprisa in sotto piedi*, which is done with sideways springs (followed by the insertion of the toe of the free foot beneath the heel of the landing foot to release it for another spring), the *Reprisa spezzata* or *broken reprise*, and the *Reprisa minuita*.

In " Patience " the steps of the *Basse danse Majeur* are done in the same manner as that laid down for " L'Amour de Moy " and " Hélas Madame " ; whereas in the *Recoupe* they are performed " broken ", as follows :—

Instead of reckoning as hitherto in *quaternions* consisting of four slow pulsations, we count in *bars* of three beats each, because the steps are now sub-divided. The pair of singles and the double take four bars each. In order to avoid all ambiguity I will describe these steps as though they started with the left foot, although it is understood that the partners will continue to use opposite feet. For the singles :—

[1] This is the Provençal spelling of the name ; Arbeau writes it " Tourdion "

HOW TO DANCE THE BASSE DANSE

On the first beat of the *first* bar advance the left foot, flat on the ground, a few inches in front of the right and on the third beat join the toe of the right foot to the heel of the left and rise on the toes. On the first beat of the *second* bar advance once more the left foot, flat on the ground, and on the third beat hop on the left toe, pointing the right foot a few inches in front. This completes the first single. During the third and fourth bars proceed in like manner, beginning with the right foot.

To make the double proceed as follows :—

On the first beat of the *first* bar step forward on the left toe and on the third beat hop on it. On the first beat of the *second* bar step forward on the right toe and on the third beat hop on it. On the first beat of the *third* bar step forward on the flat of the left foot and on the third beat join up the toe of the right foot to the heel of the left. On the first beat of the *fourth* bar advance again the left foot and on the third beat hop on the left toe. This completes the left broken double, of which the right is the counterpart. Caroso in his second treatise (*Nobilita dei Dame*) describes various ways of elaborating the doubles. In the recoupe they should be done lightly ; and as the dancer hops on one foot the other should be raised a little forward with pointed toe. All these movements must be small and undulated ; on the side of the stepping foot, the hip and shoulder should be a little advanced and the head turned in that direction.

The Broken Reprise : Turn towards partner. The man, on the first beat of the *first* bar, steps sideways in retreat with the right foot flat on the ground and the knees bent. On the third beat of the *first* bar he slides the toe of the left foot behind the heel of the right and rises on the toes. On the first beat of the *second* bar he again steps sideways in retreat with the right foot and on the third beat he slides the toe of the left foot in front of the right. On the first beat of the *third* bar he once more steps sideways in retreat with the right foot, remaining with both knees slightly bent during the three beats. On the first beat of the *fourth* bar he slides up the left foot to join the right in the third position (right), rising on the toes with straightened knees, and on the third beat he sinks both heels.

The lady simultaneously performs the same actions as the man, using the *opposite* feet.

The branle can also be broken by doing four inclinations instead of two, in the manner prescribed by Arbeau in "Jouissance vous donneray", rocking the feet and swaying the body, but with a lesser movement than when the branle is done gravely.

Next follows the *tordion* (called by the Italians *tordiglone*), which closes the dance.

The tordion in its pristine state is a cinque-pace. In later times it became much elaborated as did also its offspring, the galliard. Both of these dances stood apart from all others in that they were based on the " cinq pas " (or five steps), whose structure produces a peculiar rhythm. Each single set consists of six minim beats twice over, using alternate feet. The first four beats have each one step, and to the fifth and sixth beats is allotted the fifth step called the " cadence ", or falling step, in the performance of which the dancer makes a high jump and lands on the sixth beat with feet in the fifth position. This climax imparts to the sixth beat a marked accent, producing the effect of a syncopation. Arbeau divides the tordion into bars of six minims. Some masters write one tordion bar as two bars of three minims, and others again as three bars of duple time ; but in practice it all amounts to the same thing, as each set of cinq pas consists of two groups of six minims (or twelve crotchets). Caroso and Negri each give a tordion of fantastic elaboration, containing many stationary figures (termed " mutanze ") of their own devising. In both examples the music contains but twelve bars of duple time and consequently these would have had to be repeated between forty and fifty times, serving the purpose of a rhythmic stimulus to the intricate footwork of the expert dancers of the period.

The tordion,[1] which completes basse danse " Patience ", however, is of the primitive type which makes use of the simple cinq-pas (or cinque-pace) in progress round the room, alternated by the wheeling or turning movement from which this dance derives its name. Indeed, I doubt whether the French ever brought the tordion up to such a pitch of intricacy as did the Italian virtuosi in this art.

At the close of the recoupe the couple should be standing facing the spectators, the lady on the right of her partner with her left hand held uppermost in his right.

THE TORDION

The Figures. In the tordion the dancers use identical instead of opposite feet, as they have done hitherto in the basse danse and its recoupe. There is no need of any salutation, this having already been performed at the close of the preceding movement ; so the dancers commence their progress round the room, first turning a quarter turn left so as to go round clockwise. Two sets of cinq pas will complete the first strain once. In the repeat, the first half should be allotted to the turning movement, which will occupy one set of cinq pas ; and the second half to one set of cinq pas in progress round the room. The second strain (first time) should begin with a new turning movement occupying

---

[1] Pierre Attaignant uses the Provençal spelling.

one set of cinq pas *en fleurets*, and be completed by one simple set of cinq pas, round the room ; the dancers should arrange their path so as to arrive in the centre facing the onlookers at the close of the strain. For the repeat of the second strain a double turning movement, consisting of ten broken steps and one cadenza each way round will make an exhilarating finish. When one passes over the cadenza at the close of the first bar, filling its place with two steps, and only makes the cadenza at the close of the second bar, this is called a " passage à onze pas ", as the first bar thus contains six steps and the second five (including the closing cadenza), making a passage of eleven steps.

The cinq pas as employed in the tordion are done in a more gentle, restrained manner than in the galliard. Even in the forward kicks the feet are advanced but a few inches and raised very little above ground level. In treating of the galliard and tordion Arbeau says : " *But the said ' tourdion ' is danced more gently and with actions and gestures less violent.*" Elsewhere he characterizes it as a galliard *danced on the ground*, which expression means that the feet remain *near* the ground with toes pointing downwards. The early tordion, being composed of simpler steps, is taken at a brisker pace than the more elaborate galliard.

Its steps should be executed in the following manner :—

The Cinq-pas Advancing. Stand with the right foot forward in the fifth position. Please note that in these dances the feet are turned only *slightly* outward at an oblique angle. On the *first beat* hop on the right foot, simultaneously raising the left foot in front, with straight knee and pointed toe : on the second half of the beat lower the left toe to the ground with the point a few inches beyond the right. On the *second beat* hop on the left foot, simultaneously raising the right foot in front : on the second half of the beat lower the right toe a few inches in front of the left. On the *third beat* hop on the right foot, raising the left in front : on the second half of the beat lower the left toe as before. On the *fourth beat* hop on the left foot, raising the right in front : on the second half of the beat lower the right toe. On the *fifth beat* press the toes of both feet on the ground in the fifth position (right), bending the knees outwards : on the second half of the beat spring into the air, scooping the left foot forward. On the *sixth beat* land on both feet in the fifth position left, thus completing the left cadenza. This terminates the cinq pas *left :* to complete the set perform in a similar manner the cinq pas *right*, using reverse feet throughout and closing the cadenza in the fifth position right. Arbeau calls the high forward kick of the galliard cinq-pas " grève ", and the moderate forward kick of the tordion " pied en l'air ". For the sake of brevity he employs these terms to include the entire step, i.e. the hop on the stationary foot and the forward kick and subsequent lowering of the moving foot. The cadenza is divided by him into *saut majeur,* followed by *posture gauche* (or droite, as the case may be) for the galliard, and *saut moyen* and *posture gauche* (or droite) for the tordion.

D   37

Arbeau's directions for the tordion cinq-pas are therefore summarized as follows :—

Pied en l'air gauche.
Pied en l'air droit.
Pied en l'air gauche.
Pied en l'air droit.
Saut moyen.
Posture gauche.

Le revers des précédents

Pied en l'air droit.
Pied en l'air gauche.
Pied en l'air droit.
Pied en l'air gauche.
Saut moyen.
Posture droite.

How to perform the Turning Movement. For the first *turning movement* the dancers face each other and the man takes his partner's right hand in his own and raises it about shoulder-level.

They then revolve round one another to the right, dancing the first half of the set of cinq pas as above. When they land on posture gauche (fifth position left), they let go hands and perform a swift half-turn right (keeping the toes on the ground) ; they thus reverse their posture to fifth position right. Simultaneously the man takes his partner's left hand in his own, holding it shoulder high, and they perform the second half of the set of cinq pas, beginning with pied en l'air, right, and revolving to the left.

The Second Turning Movement. A pleasing variation can be introduced into the second turning movement by cutting the steps into fleurets. A fleuret takes two beats, the first being occupied by two half-steps, and the second by a whole step. Therefore two fleurets and one cadenza will fill six beats, to be repeated with reverse feet for the second group of six beats. In these *half* steps the stepping foot advances a few inches so that its heel arrives at the middle of the other foot. They are made lightly on the toes, and the other foot simultaneously springs forward raised about two inches from the ground. The ensuing *whole* step advances a foot's length, landing on the flat of the foot, and the other foot is immediately raised forward about four inches from the ground with straightened knee and pointed toe. This is one fleuret. In performing this variation the dancers should link arms, holding the other arm upward and outward, bent at the elbow and at the wrist. Proceed therefore as follows :—

Link first the right arms and revolve to the right. On the *first beat* make a half-step left, raising the right foot ; then a half-step right, raising the left foot. On the *second beat* make a whole step left on the flat foot, raising the right a little higher than before. On the third and fourth beats perform the same series of movements, stepping first with the right foot. This completes two fleurets (left and right), at the close of which the left foot will be raised forward. In order to perform the left cadenza, lower the left toe in line with the right heel and, as you jump, scoop it forward so as to land in the fifth position left (posture gauche). Let go arms and perform a swift half-turn right, reversing the posture to fifth position right. Linking left arms, now perform the second set of two fleurets and cadenza with reverse feet, revolving to the left. This variation would be termed by Arbeáu " cinq pas racoursis ".

The Third Turning Movement. Link right arms and perform your passage of " onze pas " revolving to the right. This will occupy twelve beats, or four bars of triple time. In the first six beats make six broken steps consisting of *twelve half-steps* on the tips of the toes, beginning with the left foot. Let go arms and in the second six beats make first *eight* more *half-steps* and a cadenza. In the first six of these eight half-steps each dancer, making a left turn, describes a separate circle ; while in the last two the partners advance towards each other. This will occupy four beats ; and in the remaining two, perform your left cadenza, landing in the fifth position left. This brings you to the half of the repeat of the second strain and constitutes the onze-pas left. For the remaining half link your left arms and go through the same movements in reverse, revolving to the left and making your separate circles to the right, concluding with the right cadenza, thus completing the set of onze-pas. At the close of the dance there will be a final chord, during which the dancers salute one another with the parting reverence termed *congé*. They then advance hand in hand (the lady on the man's right) to salute the company and the man then leads his partner to her seat with the accustomed courtesies.

BASSE DANSE " PATIENCE ". À XX

Adapted for Keyboard from the Lute setting.   Pierre Attaignant (*Dixhuit basses danses*), *1529.*

Steps for the recoupe or light
movement, termed by Arena
"La Moitié à XII."
b. d. r. b., ss. d. d. d., r. d. r. b.

DANCES OF ENGLAND AND FRANCE

HOW TO DANCE THE BASSE DANSE

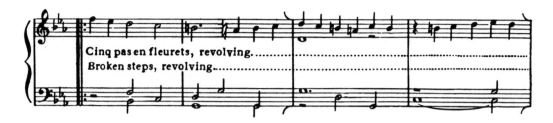

BASSE DANSE "JOUISSANCE VOUS DONNERAY"

According to Arbeau's directions the singles and doubles of this latter-day basse danse are done stepping on the accented beats as in a pavan. For the singles proceed as follows :—

Bending the knee of the stationary foot, step with the other foot flat on the ground ; rise again on the toes as you transfer your weight on to it. On the second beat join the other foot to it in the first position, sinking the heels at the close of the beat. The second single is done on the third and fourth beats with reverse feet. For the double : On the first beat, bending the knee of the stationary foot, step with the advancing foot flat on the ground : rise on the toes as you transfer your weight. On the second beat step with the reverse foot on the toes and sink the heels at the close of the beat. On the third beat step again with the first foot flat on the ground, rising as you transfer your weight ; and on the fourth beat join the other foot to it in the first position and sink the heels. Perform the diminished *reprise* as in the preceding Provençal basses danses.

Arbeau recommends that the man should make the reverence with the right foot instead of the usual practice of making it with the left.

HOW TO DANCE THE BASSE DANSE

BASSE DANSE "JOUISSANCE"

Set for Keyboard by Rudolph Dolmetsch.　　　　　*Orchésographie, 1588.*

R.b.ss.d., r.d.r.b.ss.d.d.d.r.d.r.b.ss.d.r.b.

45

DANCES OF ENGLAND AND FRANCE

Here the couple turns left and, describing a semi-circle, returns to the foot of the dance.
Retour de la Basse danse. b.d.r.b.d., r.d.r.b.ss.d.

HOW TO DANCE THE BASSE DANSE

The speech of Love :—of the orderly motion of the fixed stars.

Stanza 35   _First you see fix'd in this huge mirror blue_
            Of trembling lights a number numberless ;
            Fix'd they are nam'd, but with a name untrue ;
            For they are moved and in a dance express
            The great long year, that doth contain no less
            Than three score hundreds of those years in all
            Which the sun makes with his course natural.

                    *   *   *   *

Measures.

Stanza 65   Not those old students of the heavenly book,
            Atlas the great, Prometheus the wise,
            Which on the stars did all their lifetime look,
            Could ever find such measures in the skies,
            So full of change and rare varieties ;
            Yet all the feet whereon these measures go
            Are only spondees, solemn, grave and slow.

                    (_Orchestra_)

48

CHAPTER III

THE ENGLISH MEASURE

PART I

WE now arrive at the transformed English basse danse of the Elizabethan period, known as " The Measure ". By a rare chance we have precise indications as to how this dance was performed. I say " a rare chance ", because sixteenth-century England provides us with no detailed treatises on the art of dancing, elaborated with technical explanations, such as were produced on the Continent. After Coplande's short treatise on " The Manner to Dance Bace Dances ", appended to his *French Grammar*, published in 1521, there occurs nothing further of this nature for forty-nine years. Then in a manuscript volume of poetry,[1] dating from the year 1570, and now preserved in the Bodleian Library, the writer by some happy inspiration has inserted three pages of directions for the performance of fifteen dances of the period. The collection comprises three pavans, seven almaines, a tordiglone (tordion), a measure, a tarantella, a coranto, and a balletto for nine dancers.

There are no indications regarding the style of performance, such directions as are given being confined to the steps in their prescribed order. As an offset to this omission we are fortunate in possessing a wealth of contemporary literary allusions. These, combined with a knowledge of similar dances as practised in other countries, tell us what we need to know concerning the style and various graces appropriate to the above-mentioned types of dance. It should be understood that although the folk dances of individual countries naturally bear a strong national stamp, dancing among the educated classes of England and western Europe developed, from the sixteenth century onwards, a cosmopolitan character. Usually, however, imported dances would become more or less modified in accordance with their new environment, but without losing their fundamental characteristics.

The great work on education by Sir Thomas Elyot, entitled *The Governour* (published 1531) contains some relevant passages on dancing as a profitable recreation. It seems appropriate to quote these with their original spelling, except where this obscures the meaning. After discoursing on the symbolical character and histrionic art displayed in the dances of ancient Greece, he says : " Also there was a kynde of daunsinge called hormus, of all the other moste lyke to that whiche is at this time used ; wherin daunsed yonge men

[1] MS. Rawl. Poet 108.

and maidens . . ." "In stede of these we have now base daunsis, bargenettes (bergamesques?), pavions, turgions (tourdions) and roundes . . ." "And for as moche as by the association of a man and a woman in daunsinge may be signified matrimonie, I could in declarynge the dignitie and commoditie of that sacrament make intiere volumes . . ." "A man in his naturall perfection is fiers, hardy, strong in opinion, covaitous of glorie, desirous of knowlege, appetiting by generation to brynge forthe his semblables. The good nature of a woman is to be milde, timerouse, tractable, benigne, of sure remembrance and shamfaste . . ." "Wherfore, whan we beholde a man and a woman daunsinge together, let us suppose there to be a concorde of all the said qualities, beinge joyned together, as I have set them in ordre."

How daunsing may be an introduction unto the first morall vertue, called prudence

"The first moving in every daunse is called honour, whiche is a reverent inclination or curtaisie, with a longe deliberation or pause, and is but one motion, comprehendinge the tyme of three other motions, or settyng forth of the foote. By that may be signified that at the begynning of all our actes, we shulde do due honour to God, whiche is the roote of prudence; whiche honour is compacte of these three thinges, feare, love, and reverence . . ." "By the seconde motion, which is two in nombre may be signified celeritie and slownesse: whiche two, all be it they seme to discorde in their effectes and naturall propreties: and therfore they may be well resembled to the braule [1] in daunsynge (for in our englyshe tonge we say men do braule, whan betwene them is altercation in wordis), yet of them two springeth an excellent vertue where unto we lacke a name in englyshe. Wherfore I am constrained to usurpe a latine worde, callyng it Maturitie . . ." "Maturitie is a mean betweene two extremities . . ."

The thyrde and fourth braunches of prudence

"The thyrde motion, called singles is of two unities seperate in pasinge forwarde; by whom may be signified providence and industry; whiche after everythynge maturely achieved, as is before writen, maketh the firste pase forwarde in daunsynge . . ."

Of the fifthe braunche called circumspection shewed in reprinse

"Comunely nexte after singles in daunsinge is a reprinse, which is one moving only, puttynge backe the ryght fote to his felowe. And that may be well called circumspection, which signifieth as moche as beholdynge on every parte, what is well and sufficient, what lackethe, howe and whens it may be provided . . ."

[1] The *branle* step in a Basse danse.

THE ENGLISH MEASURE

Of the sixte, seventh, and eighte braunches of prudence

" A double in daunsinge is compacte of the nombre of three, wherby may be noted these three braunches of prudence ; election, experience, and modestie. By them the saide vertue of prudence is made complete, and is in her perfection . . ." " And thus I conclude the last parte of daunsinge, whiche diligently beholden shall appiere to be as well a necessary studie as a noble and vertuouse pastyme, used and continued in suche forme as I hiderto have declared."

To my mind the above discourse presents a perfect picture of the dignified grace and serenity of the ancient basse danse.

Let us now consider its later development in Elizabethan England where it became known as the " measure ".[1] Although in its inner construction it had undergone considerable modification, it still retained its fundamental character. This is revealed in the reflections of Beatrice in Shakespeare's *Much Ado about Nothing*, concerning wooing, wedding, and repenting : " The first suit is hot and hasty, like a Scotch jig, and full as fantastical ; the wedding, mannerly-modest, as a measure, full of state and ancientry ; and then comes repentance, and, with his bad legs falls into the cinque-pace faster and faster till he sink into his grave." The last part of this comparison has puzzled certain writers on this subject ; and I have seen the question put, " How could repentance dance the cinque-pace faster and faster if he had bad legs ? " In reality this passage is an obscure play upon words, relating to the names of the *five steps* or *cinq pas*. The cinque-pace was the primitive galliard, without the later elaborations and gymnastic feats which weighted it and retarded its swift movement. The fundamental *five steps* consisted firstly of four " zoppetti " or *limping hops*,[2] wherein the dancer hopped on one foot and held the other in the air, bringing it down after the beat as though limping ; while the fifth step, which occupied the fifth and sixth beats in a galliard bar, was the " cadenza " or *falling step*, composed of a jump from which the dancer landed with feet parted, in the second position. The simple cinque-pace went at a brisker pace than the embroidered galliard, but probably the expression " faster and faster " is intended to convey the idea that he is caught fast beyond hope of escape. Hence we can appreciate the subtlety of the above analogy, characterizing the three types of dance.

[1] Latterly the name *Measure* also denoted the Pavan and Almayne, as they superseded the Basse danse.   [2] From zoppare—to limp.

PART II

How to Dance the Measure

Number three of the dances detailed in the Elizabethan MS., mentioned at the beginning of this chapter, is called " My lord of Essex measure ". There is no music given with any of the dances, but some of this music exists in contemporary musical MSS. Although we have no record of a measure identified with the Earl of Essex, we have nevertheless a very beautiful measure in a manuscript of lute music of precisely the same date, namely *Giles Lodge Lute Book,* 1570 (now in the Shakespeare Library at Washington, U.S.A.). The music of this piece, which is entitled simply " A Measure ", happens to fit the dance of my lord of Essex, as though they were made for each other ; so I have taken advantage of this happy coincidence to join the two together.

The steps are : a double forward, one single back four times ; two singles sideways, a double forward, reprise backward.

These should be performed as follows :—

The man holds his partner's left hand in his right and, facing the onlookers, they make obeisance. Then turning towards each other at an oblique angle they make the reverence, the man with his left foot and the lady with her feet joined as described for the basse danse.* This reverence will be performed before the music of the dance begins, except that the musicians should play the while either an opening chord or four bars of introduction. The partners will use *opposite feet throughout ;* and I will describe the steps as done by the man, it being understood that the lady uses the reverse foot.

The Double : On the first beat bend the knee of the right foot and step with the left flat on the ground ; then rise on the toes at the close of the beat. On the second beat step with the right foot on the toes with straightened knees, sinking the heels at the close of the beat. On the third beat step once more with the left foot flat and the right knee bent, rising at the close of the beat ; and on the fourth beat join up the right foot with the left (on the toes) in the first position and sink the heels at the close of the beat. As you step with the left foot, advance the left hip slightly and turn the head towards the lady.

The Backward Single : This is a slow-tempo single in the nature of a semi-reverence (*révérence passagère*), and occupies four bars or beats. On the first beat step backwards with the right foot flat and bending both knees. On the second beat transfer the weight on to the right foot, straightening the left knee. On the third beat join the left foot to the right, in the first position, rising on the toes of both feet with straightened knees ; and on the fourth beat sink both heels.

Sideways Singles : These are ordinary singles occupying two bars each, but done sideways. On the first beat, bending the right knee, step sideways with the left foot flat on the ground, rising on the toes at the close of the beat. On the second beat join the right foot to the left in the third position on the toes, sinking the heels at the close of the beat. This takes you away from your partner, though you continue to hold hands, lowering them slightly. On the third and fourth beats, perform the second single with the right foot, converging towards partner and raising her hand a little. It adds grace to these sideways singles if the hip is a *little* raised on the side towards which you step.

THE ENGLISH MEASURE

These things depend upon the grace and suppleness of the dancer and should not be exaggerated.

The Succeeding Double : This is a forward double starting with the left foot and closing with the feet joined in the first position.

The Reprise : This should be a broken reprise smoothly performed. Turn a quarter-turn on the toes so as to face partner and on the first beat step sideways with the right foot in retreat, keeping the foot flat on the ground : at the half-beat join the left foot to the heel of the right in the fifth position right, rising on the toes. On the second beat step again with the right foot flat : at the half-beat join the left in front of the right in the fifth position left, rising on the toes. On the third beat step again with the right foot, keeping it flat throughout the beat. On the fourth beat join the left foot to the right heel in the fifth position right, rising on the toes ; and at the half-beat make a quarter-turn left and sink the heels. The second pair of sideways singles starts with the right foot and the succeeding forward double also. For the final reprise, turn a quarter-turn on the toes towards the lady and perform the reprise exactly the same as the first time. You will need to take very small steps in making the sideways singles so as not to collide with your partner when converging. At the close of the dance there should be a final chord, prolonged while you and your partner perform the parting reverence called *congé* towards each other. Then, turning towards the assembly, you both make obeisance, after which you lead your partner to her seat.

   * *Note.*—The lady may perform her reverence like the man, but with opposite foot.

A MEASURE

Set for Keyboard·by Arnold Dolmetsch.   *Giles Lodge Lute Book, 1570.*

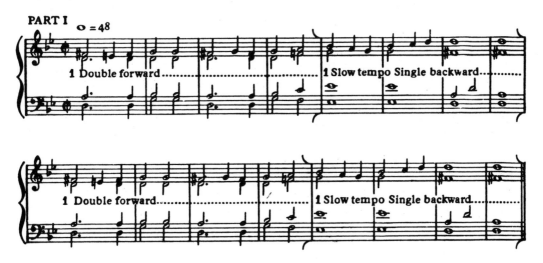

The history of the Italian basse danse is of equal importance with that of France ; and I hope to treat of it in a second volume of this work, devoted to the study of dances of Spain and Italy from 1450 to 1600.

CHAPTER IV

THE BRANLE

THIS dance derives its name from the French word " branler ", to swing from side to side, since the steps of the branle go alternately from left to right. The English converted the name into " brawl ", and drew false analogies therefrom. In Italy it was called " brando ", and as such became considerably diverted from its original character. In Spain its name was " bran " ; but it does not appear to have gained a footing in that country. It is amusing to note that in a Spanish-French Dictionary of the last century in my possession (Martinez Lopez*) we read : " Bran de Inglaterra—*ancienne danse espagnole.*"

France is the native country of the branle ; and if we include the various *rondes* that became incorporated therewith, this dance may be reckoned as of great antiquity. Indeed, one can never say when a dance *began*, because it has usually evolved from something similar bearing another name. It is only with regard to an imported dance that a date can be ascribed to it in its country of adoption.

Another feature of the branle, besides its sideways movement, is the linking of the row of dancers by the holding of hands or hooking of fingers, so that they form a chain or a circle. Apart from Antonius de Arena (1536), almost our sole source of information about the branles is Arbeau ; but, since he gained his knowledge of dancing in the province of Poitou, the true home of the branle, his teaching on this subject is entirely reliable and practical. When the branle became very fashionable it spread all over France and into adjacent countries. Arbeau provides us with an enormous variety, from the primitive types to the latest " branles morgués " or mimed branles, which were used as ballets in the court masques and thence spread to other parts of France. Among these he mentions the " Branle de Malte ", invented forty years previously, in which the dancers were attired in Turkish costume and interspersed their circular dance with the miming gestures and detached turning movements.

Antonius de Arena's information on the subject of the branle is scanty. He mentions the branles doubles, the branles simples, and the branles découpés, these last being devised for the recreation of the young people.

From Arbeau we learn that the branle is set to the same duple time as the pavan and the basse danse. We find later, however, that there are two exceptions to this rule, namely the *Branle Gay* and the *Branle de Poitou*, which go to triple time and are indeed gay and charming. *And you must understand,*

* Abridged edition.

he continues, " *that the branles are danced sideways and not stepping forward.*" The *branle double* is composed of doubles made alternately to left and right and performed smoothly and sedately without hopping. This and its companion the *branle simple* are the gravest among the branles and were considered specially suitable for the old people. They were followed by the *branles gays* for the young married couples, and the *branles de Bourgogne* for the youngest members of the company. All, however, could join in these lighter dances at their pleasure. Arbeau says on this point : " Et néantmoins tous ceulx de la dance, s'acquittent du tout comme ils peuvent, chacun selon son age, & la disposition de sa dexterité." [1]

The pupil Capriole objects that if the dancers confine themselves to making doubles alternately to left and right they will always remain in the same place. Arbeau replies that, to obviate this, they make the left double with wider steps than the right and thus gain ground leftwards. He mentions, however, another expedient, namely, that in some localities they make, in place of the right double, a reprise or a branle step. If he means the *third right* double this brings us into line with Arena, who says :—

> " Sed branlos duplos, passus tibi quinque laborent ;
> Tres fac avantum, sed reculando duos."

(But the *branles doubles* make five steps for thee ; make three advancing, but two retreating.)

The *branle double* (or *branle commun*) was set in strains of six bars, thus allowing us, as Arena directs, to make three doubles to the left and two to the right (in alternate sequence) and, in place of the sixth double, to put first a diminished reprise in the Provençal manner and, at the repeat, a branle-step. This device allows the file of dancers, moving sideways, to make its way at a reasonable pace round the room or along some open place.

For the music I have chosen a beautiful example of the " branle commun " from the keyboard settings of dance tunes published by Pierre Attaignant (1530). Arbeau also mentions another possible variation as a close, consisting of three kicks and a pause ; but, as he himself has remarked previously : " On a toujours estimé que le plus gravement et pesamment que l'on peult dancer les branles doubles c'est le meilleur ", we will take his advice and leave the sedate and formal branle double without further embellishment.

How to Dance the Branle Double (otherwise termed Branle Commun)

Taking your place hand in hand among the file of dancers with your lady on your right, make your reverence during the opening chord. This will be a less formal reverence than in the basse danse, to last the length of the chord. Note that in the branles all the dancers use identical feet.

[1] *Orchésographie*, 1588.

THE BRANLE

The Left Sideways Double : Standing with feet joined in the first position, step sideways, on the first beat, with the left foot flat on the ground. On the second beat, bring the toe of the right foot a little way behind the heel of the left, rising on the toes. On the third beat step again sideways with the left foot flat on the ground, and on the fourth beat join the right foot to the left in the first position, rising on the toes, and sinking on to the heels at the close of the beat, ready to perform the right double. This is done in the same manner as the left double but in reverse motion, stepping with the right foot on the first beat.

The Diminished Reprise : The sideways travelling of the diminished reprise is brought about by the alternate opening and shutting of the heels through the movement of the heel of one foot and the toe of the other.

At the beginning of Chapter III the five normal positions of the feet are illustrated, the first being that in which the heels are joined and the toes opened outwards at an oblique angle. All the *normal* positions have their counterpart in the *false* positions, wherein the toes converge and the heels diverge. The *false* positions are merely transitory and the dancer never rests thereon.

The diminished reprise thus consists of the rapid alternation of the *normal* first position with the *false*. To travel leftwards, move first the left heel and the right toe, producing thereby the *false* first position : next move leftwards the left toe and the right heel which restores the normal first position but removed some few inches further to the left. This constitutes one *double twist*. The dancer makes as many of these as can conveniently be fitted into the four beats. The smaller the movement, the more he can produce, as in a dextrous musical trill, while covering the same distance as do those who make larger and slower movements. When the file includes dancers of various degrees of ability, it is best to regulate the frequency so as to accommodate the less skilled, thus producing an effect of ordered progression. The slowest movement would constitute one double twist to a beat. This is performed with head and body held erect and all motionless save the feet. The entire reprise is made to the left in order to prevent a return swing to the right.

The Branle Step : This is made in Arbeau's manner with the double movement. On the first beat the man sways to the right as though bowing to his own partner ; on the second beat he bows to his left-hand neighbour ; on the third beat again to the right, and on the fourth beat to the left. This completes the step. The lady reverses the direction, swaying alternately left, right, left, right. The effect of this step discreetly performed by a long file of dancers is very impressive.

The beats of a branle double go at approximately twice the speed of those of a basse danse. Arbeau measures them in semibreves, of which there are four to the composed step (constituting one bar). For the convenience of present-day performers, however, I propose to halve the notational values in the following

57

musical examples, and so avoid producing a false impression of slowness of tempo. The minim therefore will represent the beat, in all normal branles.

The *branle simple*, according to Arbeau, follows the branle double in a suite of branles. It owes its name to the peculiarity that every left double is countered by a right single (the single is termed " simple " in French). Every second right single may be broken into three low kicks (*pieds en l'air*). These low kicks which are followed by a pause, produce the effect of marking time in a light, springy manner, the kicking foot being neatly pointed, with the knee held straight.

The Steps : Perform the left double as in the branle double (or commun). For the right single : On the first beat step sideways with the right foot flat on the ground and on the second beat, join the left foot to it, rising on the toes and sinking again. For the three kicks : On the *first* beat transfer the weight springily on to the right toe and kick with the left : on the second half of the *first* beat, lower the left toe to the ground and, transferring the weight on to it, kick with the right. On the *second* beat, transferring the weight on to the right toe, kick once more with the left ; and on the second half of the *second* beat pause, holding the left foot poised in the air ready to start the next left double. This accomplishes the three " pieds en l'air ".

BRANLE COMMUN

Pierre Attaignant.

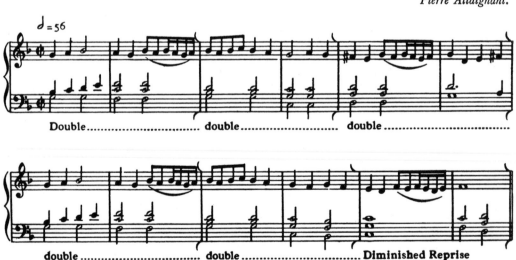

Double................................. double................................. double ....

double................................. double .... **Diminished Reprise**

58

THE BRANLE

Double .... double .... double ....

double .... double .... Branle ....

Double .... Continue the same sequence of steps throughout

Repeat
as often
as desired

59

DANCES OF ENGLAND AND FRANCE

BRANLE SIMPLE

Set by Arnold Dolmetsch.

Orchésographie.

Left double .... Right single

THE BRANLE

THE BRANLE GAY

This dance well justifies its name. Although its construction is simple, the effect that it produces when a long file of dancers, stepping with dainty precision, winds its way in and out and round about, is gay and fascinating. The tune which Arbeau gives us brings out this character better than any other that I know. The branle gay is divided by Arbeau into bars of six minims which, in accordance with the plan of halving the time values, becomes for us six crotchets to the bar (with the time signature $\frac{6}{4}$).* Technically the branle gay is not a true branle, since there is no left and right swing, the movement travelling continuously leftwards.

The Steps : The dancers, holding one another lightly by the finger-tips (shoulder high) and turning obliquely towards the left, execute, during the first half of the bar, three springy little steps on the toes, starting with the left foot ; and simultaneously with each step point the reverse foot forward a few inches from the ground (pied en l'air). On the fourth beat they step with the right foot, this time subsiding on to the flat of the foot, at the same instant advancing the left foot with a high kick (grève). The grève or high kick in a branle would be about knee-high. The left foot is thus held in the air while the dancers rest on the flat of the right foot during the remainder of the bar. The same series of steps is repeated throughout the dance, and may be summarized as :—

First half : (springing steps) *left, right, left.*
Second half : (falling step) *right,* followed by a pause.

When the kicks are made they are directed obliquely leftwards in conformity with the attitude of the dancers. At the close of the dance they may wind their way out or else form either a circle or phalanx for the succeeding branle, which would be the *branle de Bourgogne*, otherwise called the *branle de Champagne*.

* For convenience in apportioning the steps these bars have been halved.

THE BRANLE DE BOURGOGNE

This dance Arbeau likens to the branle double in that its *basic* step, which is the double to left and right, is identical therewith. He says, however, that the music is played at a brisker pace and in a lighter style (" mais ladicte mesure est plus legière et concitée "). This would evoke a corresponding lightness in the dancers' steps, as opposed to the mysterious solemnity of the branle double. He also tells us that it is customary to end each double with a high kick (grève) or a low one (*pied en l'air*) as preferred, in place of the usual joining of the feet in the first position. Arbeau's tune for the branle de Bourgogne consists of two bars of music, to be repeated for as long as the dance shall last. This short theme (even though it be garnished with variations), taken in conjunction with the unvaried simplicity of the steps, seems to me somewhat perfunctory for a dance so light and gay that it was adjudged especially suitable to the youngest members of the company. I will therefore give an alternative tune from among those published by Pierre Attaignant.

BRANLE GAY

Set by Arnold Dolmetsch.

Orchésographie.

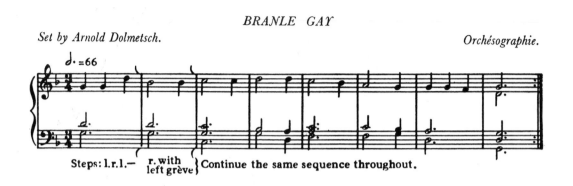

Steps: l.r.l.— r. with left grève } Continue the same sequence throughout.

BRANLE DE BOURGOGNE

Pierre Attaignant.

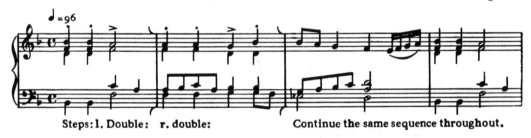

Steps: l. Double: r. double: Continue the same sequence throughout.

THE BRANLE

Beyond the four ceremonial branles, customary to the opening of the dance in Arbeau's day, we are indebted to him for a wealth of " branles sautés ", " branles coupés ", and " branles morgués ". From among these I will present a collection of the most individual types, whose interest and fascination claim a permanent place in our affections. Those who desire yet more branles will find them in the English translation of Arbeau's *Orchésographie*, by Mr. Cyril Beaumont, Charing Cross Road, London. There is also the well known French reprint with explanatory introduction by Laure Fonta (Paris, 1888), and a German translation by Czerwinski (Danzig, 1878). Of the original work few copies remain in existence. Happily one of these is in the British Museum, and I was thus able to compare with it the Laure Fonta reprint and to amend a defect in this otherwise admirable edition. This defect is due to a misconception on the part of the printer, occurring in this wise : In order that the student should easily understand which notes of the music coincide with the movements of the dancers, Arbeau sets out his tunes *vertically*, but writes out the detailed steps *horizontally* opposite to the appropriate notes. This device causes some irregularity in the spacing of the lines of text. The uncomprehending printer has therefore corrected this uneven spacing and, by rearranging the lines frustrated the object of Arbeau's invention.

None of Arbeau's musical examples are harmonized except that of the pavane, " Belle qui tiens ma vie, Captive dans tes yeux," the which is written out horizontally in a four-part score for voices. The basse danse tune, " Jouissance vous donneray," is likewise written horizontally in order that it may be accompanied by its rhythmic drum beats.

BRANLES SAUTÉS

The *branle de Bourgogne* is succeeded by the first of the hopped branles, " *branle du Hault Barrois.*" [1] This remarkably energetic branle never allows the dancers an instant's rest from their perpetual hopping, combined with expressive movements of the arms and shoulders. It is in the nature of a rustic dance and was ordinarily danced by " les vallets et chamberières, et quelquesfois par les jeusnes hommes et damoiselles quand ils font quelques mascarades desguisez en paysans et Bergiers." . . .

Equally energetic and of superior design is the branle de la montarde. Of Arbeau's description of this very ancient dance I offer the following translation :—

Formerly we used to dance a branle morgué, which they named montarde, which was danced in duple time with hops (" petits saults "), like the hault-barrois, going always towards the left, without diverting to the right. The dancers are in equal numbers of men

[1] Spelt by P. Attaignant " Hault Berroys ".

and women ; one of the men leads at the head ; one of the women holds the tail and they dance together four doubles to the left. Which done, the first makes a turn (a pirouette), separating himself from the others ; then the second makes a turn, approaching the first ; then the third makes a turn approaching the second, and thus consecutively all those of the dance make each one his turn. And when the last has made his turn the first makes a haye,[1] *passing in front of the women and behind the men and puts himself at the tail, taking the hand of the last woman : and while he makes this haye the others (before and behind whom he has passed) all rejoin hands and repeat the branle as at the beginning. Thus doing, she who was the second finds herself the first, and she must do as did the first at the beginning, and thus shall lead the first and the last each in his turn : and when the last woman has come to priority, and that she has made her haye, she finds herself last as at the beginning. Then the players of instruments terminate the branle, of which here is the tablature.*

How to Make the Steps and Evolutions

This branle accommodates comfortably twelve dancers, but can be done with a minimum of eight. Its leftward path should be circular, with a gap left between the first and the last dancer, as in the foregoing picture of the angels dancing in Paradise. The opening movement consists of four consecutive *left doubles* during which the dancers hold hands. These doubles are performed lightly, treading on the ball of the foot and following each step with a rebounding hop, thus : On the *first* beat make a sideways step with the left foot ; and, at the half-beat, hop on it ; on the *second* beat approach the right foot to it with the toe a little behind the left heel ; and, at the half-beat, hop on the right toe ; on the *third* beat step again with the left foot ; and, at the half-beat, hop on it. On the *fourth* beat join the right heel to the left with a smart tap (always treading on the ball of the foot) ; and on the half-beat hop on the right toe. This little tap of the right heel against the left helps to give precision to the close of the double and to launch the left foot outwards, poised ready to begin the next double sharp on the beat.

The Turning Movement : The steps of the turning movement consist of one double which is done spinning round in pirouette fashion, as follows : At the close of the *fourth* double in the opening strain the dancers come to rest in the first position (instead of hopping and extending the left foot sideways). They let go hands and the leader, raising his right arm curved inwards towards his head, and extending the left arm downwards and outwards, throws all his weight on the right toe ; and, with a little outward whisk of the left toe, to gain impetus, spins round to the right on the ball of the right foot. On the second beat he substitutes the left foot and continues spinning in the same

[1] This expression is derived from " la haye ", the popular French name for an artificial hedge or hurdle, formed of upright wooden stakes interlaced with transverse strands consisting of thin supple stems.

A Medieval Basse Danse.
Liber Chronicarum Mundi, 1493.

Ritual Dance of Dervishes.
Engraving after C. N. Cochin, 1789.

[face p. 64

direction. On the third beat he substitutes the right foot and continues spinning round ; and on the fourth beat he comes to rest with feet joined in the first position and sinks to the flat of the foot. While spinning he must arrange to travel leftwards away from the rest, but along the same path ; so that when he comes to a standstill he is facing front about a body's width distant from the other dancers. The direction in which he travels is controlled by the position of the stepping foot each time he poses it (left and right alternately). One cannot give an exact rule because it depends on the speed of revolution, the young people usually revolving at a faster rate than the older ones. The strain of music devoted to the turning movement is of one bar's length and must be repeated as many times as there are dancers, as the whole step is the equivalent of one double, occupying one bar for each dancer. As soon as the leader has performed his turning movement, he is followed by the second dancer who comes to rest beside him and so on right down the line till the figure is completed.

Next comes the Haye Figure : The leader faces round, with a half-turn on the right toe ; and while the rest of the file dance the plain branle movement of four left doubles he makes the interlacing pattern called the haye.

Using the same hopped doubles (which allow rapid progress), he passes, face to face, the first woman ; then, with a quarter-turn to the right, he edges between her and the next man, whom by making a quarter-turn left, he passes back to back ; and again, with another quarter-turn left, he edges between the man and the next woman, thus continuing until he arrives at the tail of the dance. This brings him to the end of the strain approximately and, taking the hand of the last woman he dances the repeat of the branle movement of four left doubles. During the haye figure, the dancers between whom he is to pass must instantly let go hands, joining up again as soon as he has passed. When the plain branle movement is completed, the first woman, now leader, once more starts the turning movement. This is followed by the haye figure which leads back again to the branle movement ; and so the sequence continues repeating itself until all the dancers are back in their original places, when the repeat of the plain branle movement brings the dance to a close.

If this branle should be performed on a stage before an audience it will be found that eight dancers are about the right number to hold the attention of the onlookers to the finish. When there are twelve, the haye figure demands deftness and promptitude on the part of all so that it may be completed in the strain of four bars ; otherwise it must be finished during the repeat of the branle movement. The hops help the dancer to gain ground.

THE SEQUENCE OF FIGURES

Opening figure : (1) Plain branle movement of four doubles : (2) The same repeated. Figure II : The turning movement. To shorten this for stage purposes, all the men may turn simultaneously leftwards, followed by the women. Repeat same to the right. This arrangement only requires the turning tune four times. Figure III : The Haye, followed by the plain branle movement.

BRANLE DE LA MONTARDE

Set by Arnold Dolmetsch.   Orchésographie.

Repeat the whole tune until all the dancers are back in their original order.

In 1928 I was teaching the branle de la montarde to a newly-formed group of dancers, when the idea arose in my mind that it was surely a very ancient dance of Eastern origin and probably held some astrological significance. Consequently, in that intention, I introduced it into a masque based on oriental legends which was produced in 1929 at the Haslemere Festival. A lady who was present remarked afterwards to a member of my group that she had witnessed a very similar dance performed by dervishes in the market place of Baghdad, after the day's business was over. This was a pleasing confirmation of a fortuitous intuition.

A further support of this idea came when, in 1934, while reading the great philosophical work entitled *A New Model of the Universe*, by P. E. Ouspensky, I came upon a description of a ritualistic dance performed at a religious festival in their college by the Whirling Dervishes of Constantinople. This ceremonial dance, though far more elaborate and demanding consummate skill from its devotees, yet shows certain features in common with its remote descendant in the west. The dance of the dervishes in Baghdad would appear to be of an intermediate type, shorn of its ritualistic character by being presented as a public spectacle. A few short extracts from the account given of this dance by Ouspensky will therefore be of interest in showing how far a dance may travel and adapt itself to its new surroundings.

THE MEVLEVI DERVISHES

" I saw them for the first time in 1908. Constantinople then was still alive. Later it died. *They* were the soul of Constantinople, though nobody knew this. . . A round hall strewn with carpets and surrounded by a breast-high wooden partition. Behind the partition, in a circular corridor, spectators. The ceremony of salutation was in progress.

Men in black robes with wide sleeves, with tall yellow camel-hair hats narrowing a little towards the top (kulas), one after another, to the accompaniment of music, approached the Sheikh, who sat on cushions with his back to the princes' box. They made low bows to him, first standing on his right, then, having taken a few steps, repeated the same bow standing on his left. . .

And what at once arrested my attention was the fact that they were all *different*. Not one face was like another. And each face at once impressed itself on the memory. . .

Again, as though from a distance, came the sound of music. One after another, without haste—some throwing off their robes and remaining in short jackets reaching to the waist and a sort of long white skirt, and others keeping their robes—the dervishes rose and with calm and assured movements, lifting the right arm, bent, the head turned to the right and the left arm outstretched, slowly stepped into the circle and with extraordinary seriousness began to turn, at the same time moving round the circle. And in the centre, his arms bent in the same way, looking at his right hand, a dervish with a short grey beard and a calm pleasant face slowly turned on one spot, shuffling his feet with a peculiar motion. All the others, some very young men, others middle-aged, and some quite old men, turned round him. And all of them turned round and moved along the circle at a different speed ; the older ones turned slowly, others, the younger ones, with a speed that took one's breath away. Some appeared as they turned to have their eyes closed ; others merely looked down, but no one of them ever touched another.

In their midst, not turning like the others, slowly walked a dervish with a grey beard, in a black robe and with a green turban wound round his camel-hair kula, with the palms of his hands pressed against his breast and his eyes lowered. He walked strangely, moving now to the right, now to the left, now advancing, now receding a little, but all the time proceeding round the circle, only sometimes passing as though from one orbit to another and back again. But he never touched any one, just as no one touched him. . . And the dervishes continued to turn round and move along the circle. Thirteen of them were whirling at the same time. Now and then one or another stopped and, slowly and calmly, with face illuminated and concentrated, sat down by the wall. Others rose and took their places in the circle . . .

Twelve years passed before I saw the dervishes again . . . And now I knew more about them. I knew a part of their secret. I knew *how they did it* . . . But in order to understand fully one must first *know why they do it.* And this cannot be told . . .

And soon the dervishes themselves disappeared. The enlightened rulers of Turkey forbade all activity to ' astrologers, fortune tellers, and dervishes '. And in the Tekka at Pera there is now a police station."

The above recital is not intended to serve as a technical exposition but to paint for us a vivid picture of this mysterious symbolical dance. The dervish in the centre slowly turning on one spot would seem to represent the sun ; and this central figure has been lost in the western dance. The other dervish who walked strangely, moving now to the right, now to the left, proceeding round the circle, sometimes passing from one orbit to another and back again, may, I imagine, be represented in our branle by the dancer who interlaces the dance in contrary motion in the figure of the haye. It would also appear that apart from the independent wanderer, twelve is the correct number in the dance.

Branle de Poitou

Speaking of certain branles which acquired great local popularity, Arbeau says : *Some branles take their denomination from the countries in which they are ordinarily practised : the Poitevins dance their branles de Poitou : the Scotch, the branles of Scotland : the Bretons, the branles which they call the triory, or passe-pied.*

Capriol says : *I wait for you to give me their tablatures.*

Arbeau replies : *Some ignorant people have corrupted the movements of the branle de Poitou, the which I do not intend to follow, and I will give you the tablature after the manner in which I used to dance it formerly with the young girls of Poitiers : This branle is danced in triple time, proceeding always to the left, without diverting to the right : I will only give you the beginning of a tune, because the rest of this tune and all the other branles* (de Poitou), *of which there are a great number, have the same movements.* He proceeds to give the first section of a very pleasing tune together with the tablature of the basic steps. His tablature in this case is a bare outline for the reason that it is noted (as with the tordion) entirely in *pieds en l'air*, making no mention of the steps which precede or accompany this movement. However, when one comes to dance it, with its continuous leftward passage, the steps come automatically, to motivate the *pieds en l'air*.

Capriol asks whether it is not customary to make use of further elaborations (*découpements*) in this branle de Poitou, saying that he has heard tell that the

"Poitevines" thus ornament the steps and produce thereby a gracious noise with their sabots. Arbeau admits that this is so and gives a formula for the cutting up of the steps which introduces further animation into this blithe and graceful dance. Instead, however, of giving us the remainder of the tune, he merely repeats the opening section.

Being desirous of performing this charming dance in its entirety, I asked Arnold Dolmetsch to complete the tune for me. This he did so convincingly that it has since been published erroneously as the authentic tune.

Steps of Branle de Poitou

This branle travels continuously towards the left, and the dancers, holding hands by the finger-tips, turn obliquely leftwards. Each section consists of three bars of six beats to the bar. The steps are as follows : —

On the first beat of the opening bar, step sideways on the ball of the left foot, simultaneously kicking the right foot forward a few inches from the ground. This is called a right *pied en l'air*. At the second half of the bar (fourth beat), step with the right foot, passing it in front of the left, and accompany the step with a left *pied en l'air*. Follow this procedure likewise for the second bar, at the end of which you will be standing on the right foot with the left raised in a *pied en l'air*. During the first half of the third bar, make three rapid *pieds en l'air* (right, left, right), as though marking time. On the fourth beat come down on the flat of the right foot, making a simultaneous left *pied en l'air*, and hold this posture until the end of the bar. This ends the first section, which should be repeated in the same manner. These steps should be performed in a dainty style, rising a little on the toes after each step, and the foot which makes the *pied en l'air* should be well pointed. *The second section* is performed in the same way except that the rising on the toes at the end of each step is replaced by a hop. The *découpements* or cut steps are reserved for the *third section* (which is a variation on the tune of the first). Its steps are followed by hops like those of the second section. On the first beat of the opening bar of the *third section* step sideways with the left foot, making a right *pied en l'air*, and on the fourth beat, step with the right foot, passing it in front of the left and making a left *pied en l'air*. On the first beat of the second bar step again with the left foot, making a right *pied en l'air*, and during the second half of the bar make three rapid *pieds en l'air* (left, right, left). During the first half of the third bar, make three more *pieds en l'air* (right, left, right), and on the fourth beat, make a final left *pied en l'air*, and hold this posture until the end of the bar. This closes the third section, after which the dance begins again and is repeated as many times as desired by all concerned.

F

DANCES OF ENGLAND AND FRANCE

BRANLE DE POITOU

Set by *Arnold Dolmetsch.*

Orchésographie.

THE BRANLE

This variety of branle has persisted in the Highlands of Scotland until recent times ; but whether it is still practised there I cannot say. Some twenty-five years ago I became acquainted with a Highland woman, brought up to speak the Gaelic language, who, after witnessing a performance by myself and children of sixteenth-century dances (including the Scotch brawl), remarked to me that the freedom and vivacity of these dances, and in particular of the brawl, reminded her strongly of those of her native county of Sutherland. The brawl, she told me, was still danced in those parts as " the brail ". I asked her whether our steps and gestures nearly resembled those of the present-day dance, to which question she replied that they did ; " only," she added apologetically, " we do more *shouting*."

Arbeau, describing this dance, says : *The branles of Scotland were fashionable about twenty years ago : the players* (musicians) *made a suite of a certain number of them of different movements which you can learn from the instruction of the said players, or from your companions. They are danced in light duple time, as you can see in the tablatures of these two following branles, which are the first and second of the suite.*

The music which he gives for these two numbers of the suite is less characteristic than are the dances ; and I suspect it to have been composed by the said players. There exists, however, in the " Straloch Manuscript " of sixteenth-century music for the lute, a piece entitled " Brail de Poitou ". It bears no resemblance to Arbeau's *branle de Poitou*, as can be seen by comparison with the foregoing example, but happily its two sections fit as by magic the two branle movements placed on record by Arbeau. Arnold Dolmetsch accordingly made a keyboard arrangement of this characteristic " brail " to enable us to present the dance in its true colours. It is amusing to think that the Scotch musicians imagined they were composing a " branle de Poitou " and the French " les branles d'Écosse ", whereas each side was merely producing its own national music.

The First Movement : The steps of the first movement are as follows : left double ; right double ; left single ; right single. This sequence is performed four times, which brings us to the conclusion of the first strain. These doubles and singles differ from any we have yet encountered, in that they close, in the typically Highland manner, with the movement termed by Arbeau " pied croisé ".

The Doubles : On the first beat, step firmly sideways on the flat of the left foot, making a light stamp. On the second beat, approach the right foot a little way behind the heel of the left, rising on the toes. On the third beat, step again sideways on the ball of the left foot (without stamping), and on the fourth beat, hop on the left toe, at the same time crossing the right foot (well

71

pointed) over the left knee. Perform the right double in like manner, using reverse feet.

The Singles : On the first beat, step sideways on the ball of the left foot and on the second beat, make the *pied croisé* by hopping on the left toe and crossing the right foot over the left knee. Make the right single in like manner, using the reverse feet.

The Second Movement : This movement is more complicated than the first, and runs as follows : (1) left double ; (2) a pair of singles (right and left) ; (3) right double ; (4) left double ; (5) right single : *pied en l'air* (right), *pied en l'air* (left) ; (6) *pied en l'air* (right), feet joined, caper. This entire sequence of steps is performed twice, which brings us to the conclusion of the second strain.

The Doubles : These are the same as in the first movement, starting with a light stamp and finishing with *pied croisé.*

The Singles : These also are the same as in the first movement.

The Cut Caper : After the last left double, it will be noted, there comes an isolated right single with left croisé which occupies the first half of the following bar. At this juncture let go hands for the cut caper, extending them downwards and outwards (the arms bent at the elbow), and complete the bar with the first and second *pieds en l'air* (right and left), springing from one to the other. The last bar starts with the third *pied en l'air* (right). This occupies the first beat and on the second beat, join feet in the third position (right) with knees bent outwards ; then spring into the ·air, passing and re-passing the feet. On the third beat, descend on both feet in the third position (right) with knees bent outwards and rise on the toes at the half-beat, sinking again on to the heels on the fourth beat. This completes the caper. When springing into the air draw the hands inwards and upwards so that they meet in front of the chest and when you descend, move them downwards and outwards, with a curved motion. This imparts grace and balance to the movement.

I gathered from my Highland acquaintance that the modern brail is usually danced by four dancers in a row. No specific number is mentioned by Arbeau. He says, speaking of branles in general : *When you shall start a branle, several others will join themselves to you, as many young men as damsels. And sometimes the one who is the last in the dance will take your left hand and thus it will be made into a round dance.*

If the dance takes place in a room and principally for the enjoyment of the dancers, a circle is the most agreeable form and can accommodate from eight to twelve dancers. But if it should be performed on a stage, then a row of dancers facing the spectators shows to advantage the ornate steps. In this case the dancer at either end should move the free arm to left and right in conformity with the direction of the steps to impart vivacity to the general movement. Such gestures should be made with the forearm, in a curved line.

THE BRANLE

BRANLE d'ÉCOSSE

Tune from Straloch MS.   *Steps from Orchésographie.*

It seems that a species of branle may still linger in Brittany, for some fifteen years ago my daughter [1] witnessed such a dance performed by men and women in the open air. The dancers, holding hands, formed a circle and, singing the

[1] Nathalie Dolmetsch Carley.

73

while, moved alternately to left and right, punctuating their steps with a swinging movement of the arms and hands. First each man would swing the hands of the woman on either side of him up to the level of his chin and down again and then each woman would do the same with the hands of the neighbouring man. Of this dance we have no documentary record, but Arbeau mentions a kind of branle peculiar to Brittany which he calls the " Triory de Bretagne " or " Passpied ", which he thus describes :—

TRIORY DE BRETAGNE

This branle is but little, if at all, practised in these times. If you should happen to dance it some day, it will be in light duple time (" mesure binaire legière ") as this tablature demonstrates : I learned it once on a time from a young Breton who lived with me as a student in Poitiers.

The tune as Arbeau gives it is fragmentary and apparently incomplete. Perhaps his fellow student hummed it so when demonstrating the steps. Arnold Dolmetsch therefore completed it for me, by developing a second strain and adding thereto a pleasing variation on the first part, which produces a satisfying whole and shows to advantage this interesting dance.

The triory de Bretagne moves continuously to the left without any compensating swing to the right. The dancers stand in a row, holding hands; but if there should be a large number of dancers who, for lack of space, prefer to form a circle, let them face outwards, so that the steps may be clearly seen. These are as follows : A left double completed by a left *pied en l'air* in place of joined feet, a sideways leap to the left, followed by three *pieds en l'air* (left, right, left), with a pause on the last one. Arbeau gives, as an alternative to the three *pieds en l'air* and pause, three *hausse talons* (right, left, right), terminated by a left *pied en l'air*. He describes the *hausse talon* as a raising of the joined heels with a simultaneous sideways twist. This should be done in anticipation of the beat, in order that the heels may come down smartly on the beat.

HOW TO EXECUTE THE STEPS

The Double : On the first beat step sideways to the left on the flat of the left foot, with knees bent slightly outwards : on the second beat, bring the right foot a little behind the left, rising on the toes with straightened knees : on the third beat, step again sideways on the flat of the left foot, kicking the right foot backwards ; on the fourth beat, slip the toe of the right foot under the left heel and project the left foot forward in a *pied en l'air*. This occupies the first bar. On the first beat of the second bar, leap sideways leftwards,[1] landing with both feet joined in the first position ; on the second beat, make a left *pied en*

[1] Naturally the leap anticipates the beat by a fraction of a second, so that the dancer may *alight* precisely on the beat.

74

l'air and on the second half of the beat, make a right *pied en l'air* ; on the third beat, make a left *pied en l'air* [1] and hold the foot in this position for the remainder of the bar. This completes the second bar. The same two bars of music are repeated, thus bringing us to the end of the strain.

The steps of the repeat are like those of the first except that, in place of the *three pieds en l'air* which follow the sideways leap there will be the three *hausse talons*, terminated by a *pied en l'air*, performed thus : After landing from your sideways leap on the first beat of the second bar, raise the joined heels and twist them to the right, coming down with a smart tap precisely on the second beat ; then raise them immediately and, twisting them to the left, bring them down again on the second half of the second beat. Raise them again and, twisting once more to the right, bring them down on the third beat. This time remain stationary on your joined feet till the fourth beat, when you make a left *pied en l'air*. This completes the second bar of the repeat. The same order of steps is followed throughout the second strain and its repeat.

Now comes the variation on the first theme, and herein it would be quite in character to " break " the heel taps in accordance with the running notes of the music. This works out as follows : The first bar of the variation is occupied as before by the left double. The second bar starts with the leap, but during the second beat, instead of tapping with the joined heels twisted to right and left, you will make four little taps (right, left, right, left), omitting the sideways twist. On the third beat you will make a final tap with the right foot, giving it a sharper accent than the others, and then remain stationary on your joined feet till the fourth beat, when you will make a left *pied en l'air*. This completes the second bar of the third strain. The same two bars of music are repeated with the same steps, bringing us to the end of the third strain. After this we go back to the beginning and repeat the same sequences of steps as many times as may be desired. When the dance comes to a close, instead of ending with a *pied en l'air*, remain with your feet joined in the first position and when the musicians play a closing chord, make your parting salutation to the onlookers in the form of a short reverence.

[1] The third *pied en l'air* should be higher than the others and can therefore be described as a *grève*.

TRIORY DE BRETAGNE

Set by Arnold Dolmetsch.   *Orchésographie.*

1. double closing with   r entretaillé   Leap: 2 kicks   1. grève.   1. double as
                         1. grève.   1.   r.

Branles Couppés

Referring to this type of branle which is light and springy, Arbeau says : *When I first came to live in this town of Lengres people only talked of dances, masquerades, and festivities. We had Master Claudin who played divinely well on the instruments and made us dance bravely. For some time now, I see nothing but trouble, besides which I am grown old and heavy. We danced in those times, among other branles couppés, the branle de la Guerre, the branle d'Aridan, the branle Charlotte, and an infinity of others.*

Branle de la Guerre

The music of this branle is spirited and gay, as is usually the case with mimic combats (such as " La Battaglia " of Negri and the Barriera).[1]   It was

[1] A mock tournament.

originally composed as a " chanson de guerre " by Maistre Clement Jannequin and printed, among a collection of part songs of this master, by Pierre Attaignant in Paris (1535). It reappeared in several later editions and was included, under the title of " La Battaglia ", in a manuscript collection of songs to the lute belonging to Petrus Fabritius (1605).[1]

The dancers form a circle holding hands. *The first strain* consists of four bars filled by four doubles, moving alternately to left and right. This is repeated, making a total of eight doubles. In *the second strain* the steps are accelerated so as to go twice as fast as before ; and thus a double occupies only two beats and a single, one. This part represents the combat and it is customary in dances of this character (if no weapons are used) for the dancers to exchange hand-clapping to suggest the clash of battle. Arbeau does not mention this feature ; but without it the dance loses its point, and one feels instinctively the necessity for this device. The steps should be short and agile like those of a fencer. They are as follows :—

The first bar consists of two doubles, left and right.
The second bar, a pair of singles and one double.
The third bar, another pair of singles and one double.
The fourth bar, one single (left) and a cut caper.

How to Dance the Doubles in the First Strain : On the first beat, step sideways on the flat of the left foot with a moderate stamp. On the second beat, approach the right foot a little behind the left, rising on the toes. On the third beat, step again sideways on the flat of the left foot (without stamping), and on the fourth beat, join the right foot to it with a little spring, landing with feet together in the first position. The right double is danced in the same manner, in reverse. At the close of the repeat of the first strain the dancers let go hands.

The Second Strain : At this point each man makes a quarter-turn right towards his partner and she a quarter-turn left to face him. At the repeat each man turns left towards the lady on his left side and each lady turns right to face the man on her right.

The Accelerated Doubles should be done as follows : On the first beat, step sideways leftwards on the ball of the left foot. On the half-beat, approach the right foot a little behind the left. On the second beat, step again sideways with the left foot and on the half-beat, click the right heel against the left heel, putting no weight on the right foot, so that it may be free to start the right double with alacrity and sharp on the beat. For the right double, proceed as in the left one but in reverse. The pair of singles is accomplished in the space of two beats. On the first beat, step to the left on the ball of the left foot and on the half-beat click the right heel against the left, putting no weight on the right

---

[1] In the Library of Copenhagen.

foot. On the second beat perform the right single similarly in reverse. The last bar starts with one left single which occupies the first beat, the remaining three beats being allocated to the cut caper. This is accomplished by starting on the second beat with two quick *pieds en l'air* (left and right), as though marking time. On the third beat make another left *pied en l'air*, rather higher ; and lowering the foot at the half-beat, make a high jump from which you must alight precisely on the fourth beat with feet joined in the third position left. If the dancers jump very high the musicians may make a slight rallentando on the third and fourth beats. While jumping, make the feet pass and repass one another as many times as can be managed. These steps (except the caper) are accompanied by *hand clapping* : At the start of each double clap your own hands together at about chest level. When making the left singles, clap your right hand against that of your opponent and when making the right singles, clap the left hand similarly against his or hers, as the case may be.

BRANLE DE LA GUERRE

Set by Arnold Dolmetsch.

Orchésographie.

THE BRANLE

.... Cut doubles: l and r: singles l. and r:

double l.   singles r and l.   double, r.   single, l. 3 kicks....... } Caper.
                                                          r. l.— r. }*

* *Note*: r. l. r. denote hops.   Kick with reverse foot.

BRANLE DE L'OFFICIAL

Of the twenty-four varieties of branle described by Arbeau, this is number twenty-three. He writes concerning it : *It is not very long since this branle was devised, the which is danced in duple time like the hault barrois : and it begins with a double to the left and a double to the right, repeated. Then the dancers proceed continuously to the left during six singles, at the completion of which, the players on instruments make the cadence* (closing bar). *Then the men take the women by the waist and make them jump and bound into the air, to alight at the said close : and meanwhile the men hold themselves solidly on their feet in order to support them ; and in these places they are much hindered who make an effort to lift up those who will not, on their side, give them any assistance* (those who do not make a responsive spring).

The branle de l'official is a lively and exhilarating dance. We may suppose it to derive its strange title from the fact that in French " l'office " denoted the kitchen quarters, where no doubt the lackeys and the serving maids disported themselves in moments of leisure with frolicsome dances which would have been considered unseemly for persons of quality, except perhaps in some masquerade.

The steps as shown in the tablature of the first strain are apportioned in relation to the tune in this wise :—

{ First-beat :	sidestep left	{ Second beat :	approach right	}
{ Half-beat :	hop [1]	{ Half-beat :	hop	} = one left
				} double
{ Third beat :	sidestep left	{ Fourth beat :	feet joined	
{ Half-beat :	hop	{ Half-beat :	hop	

[1] Called by Arbeau " petit saut ".

79

DANCES OF ENGLAND AND FRANCE

And the same sequence is followed with reverse feet for the right double. It appears unlikely that Arbeau had ever tried out his tablature for this branle, which was one of the latest of the " branles couppés " ; and as he has informed us, he had by now grown old and heavy. In practice it will be found (taking the left double for example) that, by this arrangement of following every step with a hop, the last hop falls to the right foot, thus precluding it from starting the ensuing right double. The best way out of the difficulty is to omit the third hop and, instead, to jump on to the joined feet on the fourth beat. The last hop then comes easily to the left foot, and so frees the right foot for the start of the right double, in which the last hop will fall to the right foot by the same device.

First Strain : How to execute the doubles according to the above directions : Tread lightly on the ball of the foot, except where otherwise directed. *Left Double :* On the first beat, step sideways with the left foot and at the half-beat, hop on it. On the second beat, approach the right foot a little behind the left and at the half-beat, hop on the right. On the third beat, step sideways with the left foot flat on the ground and on the fourth beat (executing a low jump), land with feet joined in the first position. At the half-beat, hop again on the *left* foot, raising the right in readiness to start the *right* double. This is performed in the same way, but with reverse feet. The first strain with its repeat requires four doubles in all. At the close of the fourth double, do not hop on the right foot, but stand with feet joined in the first position, ready to start the second strain. The first three bars of the second strain are filled by the six left singles. They are performed as follows : On the first beat, step sideways on the ball of the left foot and at the half-beat, hop on it. On the second beat, join the right foot to the left in the third position left, and at the half-beat hop on the right foot. This completes the first left single. Make the other five in the same way ; but at the close of the last, omit the hop and (remaining with feet joined), the man, at the half-beat, turns a quarter-turn right towards his partner. The lady simultaneously makes a quarter-turn left on her *right* toe (so as to face the man), and brings the left foot round into the third position left. The fourth bar starts with two *pieds en l'air*, left and right, during the first beat. On the second beat, both partners lower the right foot, joining it with the left foot in the first position and then the man, taking his partner by the waist, throws her up into the air, she helping with a simultaneous spring. On the third beat she alights on the toes in the first position, bending the knees outwards and straightening them again. On the fourth beat she sinks the heels. The repeat of the second strain is done in the same manner. The dance then returns to the beginning and is repeated as many times as may be desired by those taking part. This branle should be danced in a circle, holding hands and facing towards the centre. For the last bar the dancers are obliged to let go hands and turn to face their partners for the high jump.

80

Saints and Angels dancing in Paradise.
Italian Painting, 15th Century.

THE BRANLE

In all dances with changing steps it is best to learn the tune by heart to begin with, after which it will help the dancer to remember the steps.

BRANLE DE L'OFFICIAL

Set by Rudolph Dolmetsch.

Orchésographie.

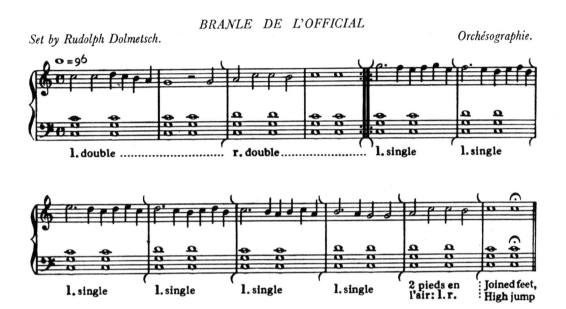

l. double .... r. double .... l. single   l. single

l. single   l. single   l. single   l. single   2 pieds en l'air: l.r.   Joined feet, High jump

How Love taught men to dance :—

Stanza 62   Then first of all he doth demonstrate plain
The motions seven that are in nature found ;
Upward and downward ; forth and back again,
To this side and to that, and turning round ;
Whereof a thousand brawls he doth compound,
Which he doth teach unto the multitude,
And ever with a turn they must conclude.

*   *   *   *

Rounds.

Stanza 64   Thus when at first Love had them marshallèd
As erst he did the shapeless mass of things
He taught them rounds and winding hays to tread
And about trees to cast themselves in rings ;
As the two Bears, whom the first mover flings
With a short turn about heaven's axeltree,
In a round dance for ever wheeling be.

(Orchestra)

81

CHAPTER V

THE PAVAN

OF all ancient dances, it is the pavan whose name is most widely known in modern times. Perhaps this is because so many beautiful pavans have been written for all manner of instruments. Indeed, far into the seventeenth century, long after the pavan had gone out of use as a dance, composers and instrumentalists remained susceptible to the mysterious charm of its solemn strains. Thomas Mace, in his book, *Music's Monument*, etc. (1687), speaking of the viol consorts enjoyed in his earlier days, says : " We had for our grave music, Fancies of 3, 4, 5, and 6 parts ; interpos'd (now and then) with some Pavans, Allmains, Solemn and Sweet Delightful Ayres ; all which were (as it were) so many Pathetical Stories, Rhetorical and Sublime Discourses. . ."

The name " Pavana " is derived from " Padoana ", an ancient dance of Padua. We have no record of its earliest form as a dance, but a study of the collection of pieces of dance music composed for the lute by Joan Ambrosio Dalza (printed by Petrucci in Venice, 1508), suggests that at that time it bore the character of an intrada. The title-page of the book announces (besides other dances) " Padoane Diverse " ; and an examination of the contents reveals nine pavans, here styled " Pavana ", each of which forms the opening dance of a suite of three, the second movement being a saltarello, and the third a piva. Soon other, more or less elaborate, forms of pavan were developed, partaking of the nature of set dances ; but nevertheless a processional form of the pavan persisted throughout the sixteenth century.

In a unique Italian manuscript of lute music dating from the close of the sixteenth century (acquired by Arnold Dolmetsch), there are a number of pieces styled " Pavana " ; but there are also others called " Intrada ", one of which is the " Lachrymæ Pavan " of Dowland, herein named " Intrada Anglicana ". This agrees with the character of the pristine pavan as revealed to us by Arbeau who says in this connection : " *Our players of instruments sound it when a young girl of good family is escorted to Holy Church for her espousal, and when they conduct the priests, the beadle, and the members of some notable brotherhood.*" A little further on he gives us this picture of the processional pavan as used on occasions of grand ceremonial : *The gentleman can dance it wearing his cloak and sword. And you others (students) dressed in your long robes, walking honestly with a staid gravity. And the damsels with a humble countenance, their eyes lowered, sometimes glancing at the company with virginal modesty. And as to the pavan it serves for the kings, princes, and grave noblemen, to show themselves on days of solemn festival with their grand mantles and robes of parade. And then the queens, princesses, and noble ladies accompany them, with the long trains of their dresses lowered and trailing, sometimes borne by damsels. And the said pavans are played by hautboys and sackbuts, who call it the grand ball and make it last until those who dance it have circled the hall two or three times : unless they should prefer to dance it advancing and retreating. The said pavans are also used when it is desired to make the entry in a masquerade of triumphal chariots of gods and goddesses, emperors, or kings full of majesty.*

On Capriol's asking what are the movements used in the pavan, the desired information is conveyed by means of the following dialogue :—

Arbeau : *The pavan is easy to dance, for it consists merely of two singles and a double walking and advancing and two singles and a double retreating and walking backwards : and it is played in duple time. And you will note that in dancing it, the said two singles and the said double of the advance begin with the left foot : and the said two singles and the double of the retreat begin with the right foot.*

Capriol : *The drum then and the other instruments make therein eight beats and measures advancing and eight measures retreating.*

Arbeau : *That is so : and if one so wishes, one makes no retreat but walks continuously forward.*

Capriol : *Does one never walk backwards in the basse danse ?*

Arbeau : *Sometimes there is such a great press and multitude of persons in the hall, that the space for dancing is much curtailed, on which account when you will have nearly reached the end, you will have to do one of two things, either to walk backwards, you and the damsel that you are leading, or else to make a conversion.*

Capriol : *What do you mean by making a conversion ?*

Arbeau : *That is to say that on approaching the end you should make the damsel to continue her onward course while you step backward as much as she will step forward,[1] until you will have turned your back to the side towards which you were previously facing.*

Capriol : *Which of the two seems to you the best to do ?*

Arbeau : *My opinion is that it were better to make use of conversion, in order that the damsel may see whither she is walking, for if she should encounter some obstacle in stepping backwards she might fall, a thing which would cause you to be blamed, and alienate you from her good graces. And this proceeding I think you should also follow in pavans, when it is desired to dance them making two or three turns round the hall.*

Capriol : *The drum beat for the pavan, is it the same as for the basse danse ?*

Arbeau : *It is duple, consisting of one minim and two crotchets in this manner :*

---

[1] By this manœuvre, although the lady steps forward and the man backward, they both describe a semicircle.

DANCES OF ENGLAND AND FRANCE

The Processional Pavan

The dancers walk in pairs, the lady on the right of the man. As many couples as desired may take part and each couple should walk about two feet behind the preceding couple. The man holds the lady's left hand uppermost in his right hand and they use identical feet throughout (not opposite feet as in the basse danse).

The steps, as we have seen, are composed of a pair of singles and one double, beginning with the left foot, followed by a pair of singles and one double, beginning with the right foot. This applies to the pavan in its primitive form, whether used in procession or by one or more pairs of dancers, advancing and retreating.

When asked by Capriol to set down in writing five or six pavans and as many common or regular basses danses, Arbeau tells him that he will find a good number of these in the dance books printed by the late Pierre Attaignant. Asked why he cannot now write them down in detail, Arbeau replies : *When you know the steps and movements of one pavan and one common basse danse, you can dance all the others : for, although they differ as to the tune and are sung and played in diverse manners, they are similar in measure. It is then for the players of instruments to learn several sorts of these : and as for you, it should suffice you to know how they must be danced, which is now easy for you, since you have learned and understood this.*

Although, as Arbeau points out, these steps are of simple construction, yet they require to be performed with the suave and supple grace characteristic of the stately pavan. There is a peculiar fascination in watching the lilting steps of a long file of dancers slowly winding its way with gently swaying motion around a hall or along some open way.

How to Perform the Steps

The Singles : The pair of singles occupies four beats in all and the double likewise four beats. The left single : On the first beat, step forward (but swerving a little towards the left) with the left foot, flat on the ground, at the same time bending the right knee slightly. On the second beat, join the right foot to the left in the first position, rising moderately on the toes with straightened knees, and sinking the heels at the half-beat. Proceed with the right single in the same manner, swerving a little towards the right, and sinking the heels after rising on the toes.

The Left Double : On the first beat step forward on the flat of the left foot. On the second beat advance the right foot a few inches in front of the left, rising gently on the toes and sinking again. On the third beat, step again on the flat of the left foot swerving to the left, and on the fourth beat join the right foot to the left in the first position, rising on the toes and sinking the heels at the half-beat.

The Right Double is performed in the same manner, but starting with the right foot and sinking the right heel after the feet are joined. When this pavan

THE PAVAN

was performed out of doors by a procession of ecclesiastical dignitaries, it may be supposed that the movements were less pronounced than when it was danced in a ballroom.

The second pavan, " La Rote de Rode," also chosen from among those published by Pierre Attaignant, is of lighter character than the preceding one and well suited to some festive occasion, or to be used as an " intrada " for the characters in a masque.

PROCESSIONAL PAVAN

Pierre Attaignant.

PAVAN " LA ROTE DE RODE "

G

If you should wish to dance the simple pavan as a *set dance* it will be found effective to have a second pair of dancers *facing you* (as Arbeau suggests with regard to the basse danse). In this way the advances and retreats appear like an interchange of courtesies between the couples and thereby gain in interest. Although Arbeau makes no mention of figures for the pavan other than the advance and retreat, it seems probable that other figures were sometimes used in this manner of pavan, as in the opening movement of certain balletti. One of these would be the crossing over into the place of the opposite couple, and another, the changing of places between the partners and subsequent return to their original position. I will therefore set out a simple pavan on these lines for those who like to dance it so, to the tune of Arbeau's lovely pavan " Belle qui tient ma vie ". The unchanging sequence of steps (namely two singles and one double) occupies eight beats starting with the left foot and is counter-balanced with another eight, starting with the right foot. So, whatever may be the figure, the same sequences of steps are employed, except for the opening salutation and the final reverence.

FIGURE I

The lady stands on the right of her partner. At the start they both turn to face each other and make the *reverence* with the left foot, which takes four beats. The next four beats are filled by two *continenze* (this is a development of the " branle " step ; but, instead of the feet remaining stationary, as in the latter they move sideways). The succeeding eight beats are devoted to the same move-ments of salutation, this time performed towards the opposite couple : These opening courtesies complete the first half of the tune.[1] The second half is filled by the advance and retreat, consisting of two singles and a double forward, beginning with the left foot and two singles and a double backward, beginning with the right foot.

FIGURE II

In the first half of this figure (consisting of two sets of eight), the opposing couples cross over into each others' places, facing round at the end by means of the movement called " conversion ", as described by Arbeau. During the second half, the partners change places (each man with his own lady) and return once again to their normal positions.

FIGURE III

This figure resembles the preceding one, in that the couples again cross over, returning to their original places ; and during the second half they repeat the interchange between partners.

---

[1] These ceremonial salutations may be omitted and replaced by a short reverence to partner and to the opposite couple. The first half of the tune would then be filled by an advance and retreat, similar to that occupying the second half.

THE PAVAN

FIGURE IV

This figure opens with the advance and retreat as performed in Figure I. In the second half of the strain, the partners face one another, the man taking the lady's right hand in his own while they perform two sideways singles (left and right). They then release hands and each describes an independent circle, turning to the left, with one left double. During the last eight bars they perform the reverence, first towards each other and then towards the opposite couple.

How to make the Reverence : During the first beat, stand with the left foot advanced ; at the second beat, draw it back a little behind the right with a semi-circular motion (still keeping the weight on the right foot and inclining the head and body). On the third beat, bend both knees and, transferring the weight on to the left foot, straighten the right knee. On the fourth beat, return the weight on to the right foot and, rising on the toes, join the left foot to the right in the first position ; then sink the heels and straighten the body again at the close of the beat.

Arm Movements : If the man is costumed in sixteenth century style and wearing a hat, he should on the first beat raise his left hand and grasp his hat by the brim. During the second and third beats he lowers the hat with an outward curving motion, keeping the inside of the hat turned towards himself. At the fourth beat he returns it to his head and firmly replaces it. The lady's left hand is raised to about the middle of her body, then lowered with an outward curve and turned inwards again at the completion of the reverence.

The Continenze : This movement, which is a modified form of the branle step, is the equivalent of " setting to partners ". It is done as follows : On the first beat, move the left foot sideways a few inches, raising the hip on that side and turning the body with bowed head towards the right. On the second beat join the right foot to it in the third position, rising on the toes with straightened knees and sinking again. This is the left continenza. The right continenza is performed during the third and fourth beats, moving towards the right and bowing towards the left. The hands move slightly in the opposite direction from that taken by the feet.

The Crossing Over Figure : When you have made the two singles (left and right) you will have approached the opposite couple. At this point the man releases his partner's left hand, and takes the right hand of the opposite lady while performing the left double. The ladies pass down the centre and the men on the outside. At the close of the left double the man releases the opposite lady's hand with a slight inclination and once more takes his partner's left hand to continue the advance with the second pair of singles. During the ensuing right double he guides his partner round towards the left while he takes a backward step to each of her forward steps. At the conclusion of the double they will have executed a half-turn and will once more be facing the opposite couple.

DANCES OF ENGLAND AND FRANCE

The changing of places between partners which occupies the second half of this figure is done as follows : The partners turn to face each other and the man takes the lady's right hand in his own while they perform the left and right *sideways* singles. During the left double, they pass on their left, letting go hands, and in executing the third step they make a half-turn left, so as to face each other for the conclusion of the double with feet joined. The return to their original positions will be made in the same manner but beginning with the right foot. The man takes the lady's left hand for the sideways singles ; and during the double they pass on their right, making a right half-turn at the third step, so as to face each other for the conclusion of the double with feet joined.

The two remaining figures need no further explanation. After the final reverence towards the opposite couple, each man leads his partner back to her seat, making a courteous half-reverence as he releases her hand.

This pavan could also be performed as a processional, or else (supposing a file of four or eight couples) by advances and retreats, intermingled at pleasure with the changing of places between partners. In this case, after the passage into each other's places with a left double, the ensuing pair of sideways singles can be followed by a right double in which each partner describes an independent circle to the right, at the close of which the partners again face one another. The return to original places is made in the same manner.

BELLE QUI TIENT MA VIE

Orchésographie, 1587.

THE PAVAN

After Arbeau has set down the music of " Belle qui tient ma vie ", Capriol remarks : *This dance of the pavan is too grave and solemn to dance solo with a young girl in a ballroom* (" pour danser en une salle avec une jeune fille seule à seule "). Arbeau replies : *The players of instruments sometimes sound it less ponderously and at brisker pace ; and by this means it takes on something of the intermediate character of the basse danse and they call it the passomezzo* (" passe meze "). *A little time ago they introduced one which they call the Spanish pavan, which is danced with ornate steps and with diversity of gesture, and because it seems to have some conformity with the dance of the canaries, I will not declare to you the manner of dancing it until we are on the subject of the said canaries ; only you will here understand that there are some dancers who cut up the double which follows on the two singles. For instead of the said double, consisting of four beats, noted as four semibreves, they make of it eight minims or sixteen crotchets and in consequence they make several placings of the feet with passages and flourishes, the which fall into the same cadence and are of the same duration of time ; and such divisions and movements of the feet lightly executed moderate the gravity of the pavan, in addition to which, after the pavan it is customary to dance the galliard, which is lively.* To Capriol's request for enlightenment concerning the details of these passages and divisions, Arbeau answers : *Your desire is nought else but to know how one may mince up a double. The good dancers, who are agile and vigorous, can make as many and as diverse divisions and flourishes as seems good to them, provided (as I have said) that they land on their final beat, the foot prepared to start the pair of singles which follows the said double. And sometimes they anticipate their passages on the second single. You will understand these passages and divisions when you shall know the diverse modes and fashions of moving the feet, of which we shall speak in describing the dance of the galliard.*

In the appropriate place (after the canaries), Arbeau treats of the Spanish pavan ; but his directions are scanty, and he only gives one figure of the dance, saying that the pupil will be able to learn the other movements at his leisure. We will therefore reserve the detailed description of the Spanish pavan for the second volume of this treatise, to be devoted to Italian and Spanish dances, and now turn our attention to the English pavan.

In England, as we have already observed, the pavan was used both in procession and as a set dance. When it figured in some impressive ceremony it would be danced with stately grace to solemn and majestic music ; but for occasions of revelry, such as a courtly masque, the processional parade of the characters would be made to a pavan of more lively type, at a faster tempo. To this latter kind of music belongs " the Lord Zouche's maske ".

The solemn pavan is clearly pictured in Shakespeare's *King Henry the Eighth*, Act iv, scene 2, wherein the visionary beings perform a mystic dance around the couch on which sleeps the dying queen. This dance, as described in the stage directions, interprets admirably the weeping strains of Dowland's " Lachrymæ Pavan ".

DANCES OF ENGLAND AND FRANCE

King Henry VIII, Act iv, scene 2.

    Sad and solemn music.]

    Griffith : She is asleep : good wench, let's sit down quiet,

                For fear we wake her : softly, gentle Patience.

    The vision. Enter, solemnly tripping one after another, six personages, clad in white robes, wearing on their heads garlands of bays, and golden vizards on their faces ; branches of bays, or palm in their hands. They first congee unto her, then dance ; and, at certain changes, the first two hold a spare garland over her head : at which the other four make reverent curtsies ; then the two that held the garland deliver the same to the other next two, who observe the same order in their [1] *changes, and holding the garland over her head : which done, they deliver the same garland to the last two, who likewise observe the same order : at which (as it were by inspiration) she makes in her sleep signs of rejoicing, and holdeth up her hands to heaven : and so in their dancing vanish, carrying the garland with them. . .*

LACHRYMÆ PAVAN

John Dowland.

[1] The word " changes " is a translation of the Italian term " mutanze " signifying the stationary variations which contrast with the " passeggio " or walking steps.

THE PAVAN

Da Capo if desired 𝄉

Congé

First and second strains: First and second verses

Flow___ tears from___ your springs. Ex-iled___ for ev-er   let me mourn, where

DANCES OF ENGLAND AND FRANCE

night's black bird her sad in-fam-y sings, there let me___ five for-lorn.

Nev-er let my woes be re-liev-ed, since pity's fled and tears and sighs

and groans my wea-ry days, my wea-ry days all joys have de-priv-ed.

First and second strains: Third and fourth verses

Down___ lights, shine___ no more! No night___ is dark e-

-nough, for those that in___ des-pair their for-tunes de-plore. Light

doth but___ shame dis-close. From the high-est spire___ of___ con-

-tent-ment my___ for-tune's thrown, and fear and grief and pains

for my de-serts, for my de-serts are hopes. Hope is___ gone.

Third strain: Fifth verse

Hark___ that in dark-ness___ dwell, learn to con-temn

92

THE PAVAN

light.   Hap - py, hap - py they that in

hell   feel   not the world's_____ des - pite._____

THE LORD ZOUCHE'S MASQUE

Anon., sixteenth century.

It is interesting to remark that the above-mentioned sixteenth-century Italian manuscript of lute music, acquired by Arnold Dolmetsch, contains besides the " Lachrymæ Pavan ", also " The Lord Zouche's Masque " which is similarly entitled " Intrada Anglicana ".

We will now consider the two English pavans, of which the steps are noted in the Rawlinson manuscript before alluded to.[1]

The first of these is a short pavan and therefore combines well with the music of " The Earl of Salisbury's Pavan ", by William Byrd, which is composed of two strains only.

The Steps : As no form of salutation is mentioned, we presume that this takes place as with the French pavan, before the dance opens, on a preliminary chord occupying the space of four beats, and corresponds to the *congé* mentioned in the dance of the visionary beings. The sequence of steps noted in the Rawlinson manuscript is as follows : Two singles and a double forward ; two sideways singles and a reprise (or retreat) backward.

THE MANNER OF PERFORMANCE

The Congé is a moderate reverence called by the Italians " reverenza minima ", and performed in the space of four minim beats. On the first of these,

[1] Rawl. Poet. 1570 ; Bodleian Library.

stand with the left foot forward, flat upon the ground ; on the second beat draw it back till the left toe rests behind the right heel ; on the third beat, bend both knees slightly, inclining the head and body, and on the fourth beat, join the left foot again to the right in the first position, straightening the knees and raising once more the head and body. The opening chord should be played in arpeggio.

The Forward Singles : On the first beat, advance the left foot a few inches, treading on the flat of the foot and bending both knees, and on the second beat, join the right foot to the left in the first position, rising on the toes and sinking again to the flat of the foot. This completes the left single in two beats. Perform the right forward single in like manner, starting with the right foot. It is in character to advance a little the hip on the side of the stepping foot. This is called in Italian " pavoneggiarsi " (to display oneself like the peacock).

The Forward Double : On the first beat, bending the knees, advance the left foot, treading on the flat of the foot ; on the second beat advance the right foot a few inches beyond the left, rising on the toes with straightened knees ; on the third beat step again on the flat of the left foot and on the fourth beat join the right foot to it in the first position, rising on the toes and sinking the heels at the close of the beat.

The Sideways Singles : These are performed in the same manner as the forward singles, except that the step is made sideways, and they start with the right foot.

The Backward Reprise : This takes four beats. On the first beat, step backward on the flat of the right foot, turning the body a little towards the right, and placing the foot so that the toe comes just behind the heel of the left foot ; at the half-beat throw the weight on to the back foot, and point the toe of the forward foot with elegance ; on the second beat, step backward similarly on the flat of the left foot, turning the body a little towards the left, and pointing the toe of the forward foot ; on the third beat, again step backward with the right foot, turning the body as before and pointing the forward foot ; on the fourth beat, draw back the left foot level with the right and, facing forward, rise on the toes and sink again to the flat of the feet. This completes the backward reprise.

How to Arrange the Figures

Figure 1 : The partners stand side by side with the lady on the right of the man, who holds her left hand uppermost in his right. After the preliminary reverence on an arpeggio chord, the couple advances with two singles, left and right, and a left double. Next follows the " retreat ", composed of two sideways singles, right and left, and the backward reprise. This concludes the first figure.

Figure 2 : The couple advances as before with two singles and a double, starting with the left foot, but, instead of performing the retreat facing the onlookers, they turn sideways so as to face each other. The man takes the lady's left hand in his own and they perform the right and left sideways singles. He then releases her hand and they retreat from each other with the backward reprise.

Figure 3 : The partners advance towards one another with left and right forward singles and a left double. When starting the double the man takes his partner's right hand in his own and they pass on into each other's places. When making the third step of the double, having now passed, they make a right half-turn on the left toe, so as again to face each other, and conclude the double by joining the right foot to the left in the first position. The retreat is made as in figure 2 except that the partners have now changed places.

Figure 4 : The advance is made as in figure 3, the partners this time changing back into their original positions. For the retreat, after making the two sideways singles, they turn to face the onlookers, and the man takes the lady's left hand in his right as at the beginning of the dance. They then perform the backward reprise as before described, starting with the right foot. This brings us to the end of the strain. The couple then bow to the audience and the man leads his partner to her seat, with the usual courtesies.

THE EARL OF SALISBURY'S PAVAN

William Byrd.

THE PAVAN

THE LONG PAVAN

The second pavan noted in the Rawlinson manuscript is entitled " The Longe Pavian ". It contains five sequences of steps, three of which are performed twice and two only once, thus fitting into a pavan of four strains with repeats. English pavans are usually composed of three strains and occasionally only two.[1] In a manuscript collection of miscellaneous music acquired by Arnold Dolmetsch, however, there occurs an English pavan, dated 1550, containing four strains with repeats. This piece, therefore, is of exactly the right length to accommodate the *long pavan*. At the close of the final strain there is written, " Finis quoth Master Newman." It has therefore become known among us as " Master Newman's Pavan ".

The sequences of steps noted for the *long pavan* are as follows : (1) Two singles and a double forward : two sideways singles and reprise back : *once.* (2) Two sideways singles and a double forward : reprise back : *twice.* (3) Two singles and a double forward : one single (and reprise)[2] back : *twice.* (4) Two singles and a double forward : two sideways singles and reprise back : *once.* (5) Two sideways singles and a double forward : reprise back : *twice.*

The Steps : The *pairs* of *singles* and the *doubles* should be performed in the same style as in the foregoing short pavan ; so also the *reprise* which, preceded by the sideways singles, forms the retreat.

The Slow Single : In the third sequence, where one single only opens the retreat, this should be performed backwards in slow tempo, occupying as much time as a pair of ordinary singles. On the first beat, step backwards with the right foot, bending the knee as though in graceful salute and on the second beat, straighten the knees ; on the third beat, join the left foot to the right, rising on the toes, and on the fourth beat, sink the heels.

The Long Reprise : In the second and fifth sequences the retreat consists of *a reprise alone.* This therefore will be a *long* reprise, occupying eight beats instead of four. On the first beat, step backwards with the left foot, with bent knee ; and on the second beat (straightening the knee), draw the right foot in front of the left, pointing the toe and putting no weight upon it ; on the third beat, step backwards with the right foot with bent knee ; and on the fourth beat (straightening the knee), point the left toe in front of the right. This completes the first half. On the fifth beat, step backwards on the flat of the left foot, so that the toe comes just behind the heel of the right, and at the *half-beat*, throw the weight on to the back foot and point the toe of the forward foot ; on the sixth beat, step back similarly with the right foot, performing the same actions ; on the seventh beat, again step back with the left foot, performing the same actions, and on the eighth beat, draw back the right foot level with the left,

---

[1] In the case of a processional pavan the music would be repeated as many times as required by the procession.

[2] Omitted from MS., but necessary to the retreat.

rising on the toes and sinking again. This completes the *long backward reprise*. Throughout this movement there is a slight turning of the body to the right or left, i.e. towards the same side as that of the backward stepping foot. This turning of the body is more pronounced when the dancers are separated than when they are dancing hand in hand.

THE FIGURES OF THE LONG PAVAN

Figure 1 : This is a short figure, consisting of one advance and retreat, and occupies the first strain once, minus the repeat. There should be an opening chord, in arpeggio, or held for four beats, during which the short reverence is performed. Then hand in hand (the lady on her partner's right) the couple advances towards the onlookers with two forward singles (left and right) and a double. This takes half of the strain, the remaining half of which is filled by the retreat, composed of two sideways singles and a backward reprise, beginning with the right foot.

Figure 2 : This figure, being double the length of the first, occupies the repeat of the first strain and the first time of playing the second strain. The couple again advances with two sideways singles and a forward double, beginning with the left foot. They then let go hands and, turning to face each other (and sideways to the spectators), perform the long backward reprise as described above. This completes the first half of the figure and the repeat of the first strain of the music. During the second half of the figure they advance towards each other with two sideways singles and a forward double, beginning with the left foot. As they approach each other the man should lift the lady's right hand in his own and (as the Italian masters say) " feign " to kiss it. He then releases the lady's hand, and they again perform the long reprise in retreat, away from each other, starting with the right foot. This concludes the second figure, and the first time of the second strain of music.

Figure 3 : The partners advance towards each other with a pair of forward singles (left and right) and a left double. When starting the double, the man takes his partner's right hand in his own and they pass on into each other's places. When making the third step of the double, having now passed, they make a right half-turn on the left toe so as again to face each other, and conclude the double by joining the right foot to the left in the first position. The retreat consists of one slow single occupying four beats and beginning with the right foot, followed by the ordinary backward reprise, beginning with the left foot. This completes the first half of the third figure and the repeat of the second strain of music. The second half of the figure consists of the same movements as those of the first half with the partners passing one another during the double and returning to their original places. This time the pair of forward singles begins with the right foot and when starting the right double, the man takes the lady's *left* hand in his own while they pass into each other's places, making

THE PAVAN

a left half turn on the right toe on the third step of the double, so as to face each other at the close. The slow single which begins the retreat, starts this time with the left foot and the reprise with the right. This completes the third figure and the third strain of music, minus the repeat.

Figure 4 : This figure consists of one advance and retreat only, like the first one, and occupies the repeat of the third strain of music. The partners advance towards each other with a pair of forward singles (left and right) ; for the ensuing double the man takes the lady's left hand in his right, as they turn to face the onlookers, advancing together. The retreat composed of two sideways singles and a reprise, starting with the right foot, is performed still facing forward hand in hand. This completes the fourth figure and the repeat of the third strain.

Figure 5 : This figure contains two advances and retreats and occupies the fourth strain and its repeat. The man takes the lady's right hand in his own as they turn to face each other for the two sideways singles (left and right) which open the figure. For the ensuing forward double he releases his partner's hand and each dancer (turning leftwards) describes a separate circle, at the end of which they meet once more face to face, and sideways to the spectators. To perform the retreat, the man takes his partner's left hand in his right and they both make a quarter-turn so as to face the audience as they begin the *long reprise*, which occupies eight beats and completes the first half of the figure. During the second half, the partners remain hand in hand, facing forward as they perform the pair of sideways singles (left and right), followed by a forward double and the long reprise (starting with the right foot) which brings them to the conclusion of the pavan. During the closing chord they make a parting reverence to the onlookers, after which the man leads his partner back to her place. At parting he will make a short reverence, which courtesy she will return before seating herself. Throughout this pavan the gestures should be dignified and ceremonious. When making the sideways singles it is good to move the free hand gently in the direction in which the foot is moving ; and with the forward singles, towards the left for a left single and to the right for a right single. The books are not precise on this point, the Italian masters merely suggesting the waving of the hand gently from side to side and the advancing of the hip on the side of the moving foot.

MASTER NEWMAN'S PAVAN
MS. in the Dolmetsch Library. 1550.

99

Finis quoth Master Newman.

The earliest pavans were usually followed by a saltarello, as may be observed in the suites for the lute of Dalza (1508), and some of those in the publications of Pierre Attaignant (1529). As the pavan gradually superseded the basse danse in England and France, it annexed the cinque-pace or tourdion in place of the saltarello as its own sequel. This dance then became modified in the process, the structural *cinq-pas* being interspersed with elaborate variations. Hence it took the name of the *galliard*, a name originally signifying a gay and vigorous dance. Indeed the *Spanish* galliard of Caroso, " gagliarda di Spagna," dedicated to the consort of the Governor of Milan (which was then a Spanish possession), is in duple time and bears no trace of the *cinque passi*.

In Italy the tourdion (tordiglione) continued to develop along independent lines as an isolated dance of some importance which rivalled the galliard in its intricate and strenuous variations, whereas the basses danses of Caroso are followed by a " sciolta " of the saltarello type.

The figures which I have indicated for the two foregoing English pavans from the Rawlinson manuscript are devised after the Italian models for this type of dance, since it would appear that the Italian-Spanish influence governs to some extent the dances recorded in this manuscript, rather than the French. Witness the name " turquylonye ",[1] evidently a corruption of *tordiglione*, " tynternelo " for *tarantella*, and " coranto dyspyne " for *corriente di Spagna*. The figures that I suggest, therefore, though by no means arbitrary, appear to me as a suitable interpretation of the plan on which the sequences of steps are arranged.

The tordiglione and the tarantella will be dealt with in the proposed Italian-Spanish companion volume to this book.

[1] The full title in the manuscript is " Turquylonye le Basse " or Tordiglione of the Basses danses.

The speech of Love :—

Stanza 34
*Behold the world, how it is whirlèd round !
And for it is so whirl'd, is naméd so ;
In whose large volume many rules are found
Of this new art, which it doth fairly show.
For your quick eyes in wand'ring to and fro
From east to west on no one thing can glance,
But, if you mark it well, it seems to dance.*

*   *   *   *

Of the planets.

Stanza 41
*Who doth not see the measures of the Moon ?
Which thirteen times she danceth every year,
And ends her pavan thirteen times as soon
As doth her brother, of whose golden hair
She borroweth part and proudly doth it wear.
Then doth she coyly turn her face aside,
That half her cheek is scarce sometimes descried.*

(*Orchestra*)

CHAPTER VI

THE GALLIARD

THOMAS Morley, in his *Plaine and Easie Introduction to Practicall Musicke* (1597), in treating of various types of musical composition, both light and serious, says : " The next in gravity and goodness unto this " (the fantasy) " is called a pavane, a kind of staide musick ordained for grave dauncing, and most commonly made of three strains, whereof everie straine is plaid or sung twice." . . . " After every pavan we usually set a galliard (that is, a kind of musicke made out of the other)." . . . " This is a lighter and more stirring kinde of dauncing than the pavane consisting of the same number of straines, and looke howe manie foures of semibreves you put in the straine of your pavan, so many times six minimes must you put in the straine of your galliard."

This practice of evolving the tune of the galliard from that of the pavan is frequently to be met with in English music of the sixteenth century, the galliard following on " The Earl of Salisbury's Pavan " being of this type.

In a publication of dance tunes for the keyboard by Pierre Attaignant (quatorze Gaillardes neuf Pavennes, etc., 1530), the first and second pavans in the book are followed each by a galliard constructed on the theme of the pavan, but apart from these, the remainder of the pavans and galliards are independent compositions. In another publication, also by Pierre Attaignant, of dance tunes set for the lute (*Dixhuit basses danses*, 1529), the fourth pavan is followed by a saltarello whose tune is similarly adapted from that of the preceding pavan. In the time of Arbeau, who is our chief authority on the pristine galliard (*Orchésographie*, 1588), the choice of galliards seems to have been entirely free of any preceding pavan.

On the subject of galliard technique Arbeau imparts a wealth of information, set out in a precise and orderly manner. On one question only is he vague ; and that concerns the part played by the lady in this strenuous dance. Fortunately this deficiency is made good by both Caroso and Negri, who supply us with full details as to the ordering of the dance from start to finish, together with a description of the type of variations (" mutanze ") wherein the lady may charm the onlookers with her light and airy grace. The virtue of the man, we learn, lies in his agility, precision, and rapidity of footwork, and his muscular strength displayed in various *tours de force*.

The dance proceeds as follows : After the opening salutation (face to face), the partners, each making a sideways left double which takes them to the opposite end of the dance, again turn to face each other, by a right quarter-turn on the third step of the double, followed by feet joined. These preliminaries accomplished, the galliard starts and will consist of the counterpassing of the partners by means of the cinq-pas, alternated with stationary variations thereon. Of these there is an immense choice from which the dancers may devise their own galliards. The galliard was sometimes danced as a solo dance by an expert man-dancer who would then make use of the most florid and spectacular variations interspersed with simple passages of cinq-pas, advancing and retreating, or describing a circle or merely revolving to right and left. Both Caroso and Negri provide us with an astonishing list of all the steps that a gentleman may employ in dancing a galliard. These include such feats as the performance of a high jump, during which the dancer makes two revolutions in the air before landing lightly on the toes, with knees bent slightly outwards *to give the better grace*. There are, moreover, some variations described whose *prestissimo* subdivisions of the steps call for considerable virtuosity from the dancer. On the other hand there are galliard figures introduced into some of the balletti for two, four, or more dancers which partake of the simplicity of the cinque-pace.

The galliards described by Arbeau are intermediate between these two extremes and, though they contain some ornate steps, these are such as any dancer of average skill may execute with a good grace.

Arbeau begins his exposition of the several types of cinq-pas by illustrating certain positions of the feet, the which are almost the same as those that later became adopted as the standard positions. Next follows a description of the half reverence (" révérence passagère "). This constitutes one of the galliard movements, in contradistinction to the formal reverence of salutation (révérence salutatoire) preceding, intersecting, or closing a dance. After this he describes the movements from which various types of cinq-pas may be composed. These consist of (1) pied croisé (crossed foot) ; (2) marque pied and marque talon (toe and heel) ; (3) the grève and the pied en l'air (the high kick and low kick) ; (4) the ruade (backward kick) ; (5) the ru de vache (sideways kick of the cow) ; (6) the posture ; (7) the saut majeur (high jump), which, when ornamented by the movement of the feet in the air, becomes the " capriole " (caper). It is either the high or medium jump, as the case may be, followed by the posture, that constitutes the *cadence* (called by the Italians " cadenza ") which closes the cinq-pas.

From the above-mentioned movements, plus the *fleuret* (flourish), the different varieties of cinq-pas may be composed. Arbeau recommends that the man-dancer, before separating from his partner in order to dance his own vigorous and flamboyant figures, should first make the circuit of the room hand in hand with her, performing his cinq-pas with gentleness and moderation. After-wards he may heighten the cinq-pas and, in front of her, may then perform with brilliance such passages as he pleases (" et alors avec gaillardise ferez tels

DANCES OF ENGLAND AND FRANCE

passages que bon vous semblera "). When the *ruade* is used in the cinq-pas, the backward kicking foot, on its return, slips the toe beneath the heel of the stationary foot, projecting it forward for the ensuing grève. This movement is called by Arbeau " entretaille " and by the Italians " sottopiede ".

Concerning the technique of the cinq-pas, Arbeau writes as follows : —

Capriol : *I have remarked that in all these movements hitherto mentioned, there is always one foot or both on the ground.*

Arbeau : *You speak truly : and certainly those which have but one foot on the ground are the more lively : but there is a movement called the jump* (saut) *which is made when the two feet are off the ground raised in the air and which is even more lively* (gaillard) : *and you should understand that there are two sorts of jumps, namely the high jump* (saut majeur), *and the hop* (petit saut) : *as to the hop it forms part and portion of the movements, and is not noted in the tablature which designates it.*

Capriol : *I do not understand what you say.*

Arbeau : *Imagine yourself there with the feet joined. If the tablature command you to make a right grève, how would you do it ?*

Capriol : *I should leave my body on the left foot and should raise the right foot forward.*

Arbeau : *The right grève would be passable so done, but it would not be gay ; that is why, instead of leaving the left foot on the ground, you must pose it afresh : and to do this, it is necessary to make a hop on the said left foot : and at the same instant make the grève with the right foot : in doing which you will easily understand that the hop is, as I told you, a part of the movement of the grève. And thus you must employ the hop in all the other steps and movements where one of the feet is raised in the air, and also you may remark, I have told you that you must both spring on to and place the feet (" jetter et poser les pieds ") : for this reason when I give you in writing the tablature of the galliard, I shall be silent about the said hop, and shall write for you only the said steps and movements since this is taken for granted and understood. . .*

Capriol : *To make then the time beats necessary to the cinq-pas, one must make four movements, then a high jump and then the posture.*

Arbeau : *That is true and when one makes the cadence, which the musicians call " clausulam " and there happen to be dancers so agile that in performing the said high jump they agitate their feet in the air ; such a movement is called capriole. . .*

Capriol : *I will willingly learn this capriole since it bears my name : but what is it that you call cadence ?*

Arbeau : *Cadence is nothing else than a high jump followed by a posture : and as you see that in musical airs the players of instruments, having played the penultimate chord, remain silent for a short space of time : then play the last chord to make a soft, harmonious close, even so the high jump, which is almost like a silence of the feet and cessation of movements, is the cause that the posture which follows it has a better grace, and is found more agreeable.*

Capriol asks whether the cadence always falls on the sixth beat and is told

104

that it is sometimes delayed and passed over until the twelfth beat. The high jump having been made only on the eleventh beat, this produces a passage of " onze-pas " or eleven steps, six in the first bar and five, including the cadence in the second. Similarly the cadence may be delayed until the eighteenth beat, producing a passage of seventeen steps ; Arbeau adds that it may even be delayed until the 24th, 30th, or 36th beat, producing a passage of 23, 29, or 35 steps ; but Capriol is advised not to overdo this delaying of the cadence, lest he should weary the spectators who would become tired of waiting for it.

Capriol requests the master to give him first the tune of a tourdion and afterwards that of a galliard. To this Arbeau replies : *The air of a tourdion and the air of a galliard are of the same kind and there is no difference except that the tourdion is danced low and on the ground to a measure which is light and quick. And the galliard is danced high to a measure which is slower and more weighty : however, you do well to ask for the tune of a tourdion ; for when the tunes are known by the dancer and he sings them in his heart with the instrumentalist, he cannot fail to dance them well : you will therefore take the following tune for all the other tourdions, of which there are numberless varieties.*

Tourdion (*Orchésographie*) :

Capriol : *I understand this air well : but I do not perceive the cadences of which you had told me.*

Arbeau : *I have distinguished for you by bars and lines the limit of the cadences, which you can reduce for yourself thus :—*

SIMPLIFICATION OF THE TOURDION AIR TO DEMONSTRATE THE RECURRING CADENCES

Capriol : *I understand it better than before ; it only remains to me to know what movements I shall perform.*

Arbeau : *Make left pied en l'air* [1] *during the first minim, for the first step. Then right pied en l'air on the second minim for the second step. Then left pied en l'air on the third minim for the third step. Then right pied en l'air on the fourth minim for the fourth step. On the rest, which occupies the place of a minim, make a medium jump, considering that it is a tourdion that you are dancing : on the last minim, make a left posture for the fifth step.*

Continuing your tourdion, change and make to the right that which you will have made to the left, and to the left that which you will have made to the right. . . .

And thus proceed for as long as the instrumentalists will continue to play, to counter-pass (permuter) *and to fall reciprocally in cadence, one time in the left posture and the other time in the right posture. . .*

The posture as *illustrated* by Arbeau approximates to the *fourth* position. The length of the galliard *step*, as given by Negri, is four fingers between the toe of the backward foot and the heel of the forward foot, and in the case of the *cadenza*, Caroso directs the dancer to alight with both feet on the ground, one behind the other. This seems to suggest rather the *fifth* position which makes a neater finish. Arbeau's description of the counterpassing in the galliard implies that the lady from time to time leaves her partner and goes to the other end of the room, where he later follows her to dance again before her his ornate steps. One wonders how she gets past him without appearing to ignore his exhibition of virtuosity and what he does while she is moving to her new position. I feel, therefore, that it is more reasonable to follow the precise directions of the Italian masters for the *simultaneous* counterpassing of the partners, who describe a shallow curve in their *passeggio* and turn to face each other, on meeting in the centre, for the first cadenza. For the second half of the cinq-pas they make a quarter-turn right, and perform their steps backwards so as to remain face to face while changing into each others' places at opposite ends of the dance. Their respective positions in this manner are only a few feet apart ; and therefore the man dancer is free to perform his spectacular variations before the lady while she reciprocates with the airy, graceful passages allotted to her by the convention of the period. Where, however, the man is not a highly skilled dancer, the partners may perform more or less identical variations between the counter-passing, according to their pleasure, in the manner of the galliard movements occurring in balletti.[2]

The before-mentioned passage in *Orchésographie*, describing the evolutions of the galliard figures, runs as follows :—

Arbeau : *Those who dance the galliard nowadays in the towns dance tumultuously, and content themselves with executing the cinq-pas and some few passages without any set plan, and do not trouble, provided they fall in cadence : so much so that many of the best passages are unknown and lost : formerly we danced it with greater discretion.*

---

[1] A *pied en l'air* (or low kick) for the Tourdion and a *grève* (or high kick) for the Galliard.
[2] The man, however, should make his steps higher and more vigorous than those of the lady.

For, after the dancer had taken the demoiselle and they had placed themselves at the end of the ballroom, they made, after the reverence, one or two turns round the room, simply walking : then the dancer released the said demoiselle, who went dancing right to the end of the room, where, on arrival, she took up her station, dancing the while in this same place : during this time the dancer, who followed her, came and presented himself before her and there performed some passage (stationary variation), turning if he so wished to the right and then to the left. This done, she would go dancing to the other end of the room, where the said dancer went dancing in quest of her, in order to execute in front of her some other passage. And thus continuing these comings and goings, the said dancer made always new passages, showing all that he could do, until the players of instruments made an end of playing. Then he made the reverence, and, taking the demoiselle by the hand, restored her to the place whence he had taken her.

It will be observed that the lady in this manner of dancing the galliard appears merely to fill the role of a figurehead, before whom the gallant may display his prowess ; and I can but attribute this indifferent attitude towards her contribution to the dance to Arbeau's exalted position on the Church, as Chanoine de Langres.

This deficiency, however, can be made up by reference to Negri, whose explicit directions leave no doubt in our minds as to the correct procedure, when the galliard is danced *à deux*. He writes : *The Cavalier then going to dance with the Lady : after he has made the reverence, and a passeggio [1] round the room, and replaced his hat upon his head and arranged his cloak and sword, with the actions aforesaid ; then, making a short passeggio together, the one to the head and the other to the foot of the dance, they begin to dance, counterpassing with the cinque-passi or other variations the one into the place of the other, facing one another : I warn you that in all the figures that are made, whether forward, sideways, or turning, the Cavalier and the Lady, are always vis à vis, with the face turned the one to the other. The same rule holds good when they will have counterpassed the one into the place of the other, deploying themselves somewhat (" con pavoneggiarsi alquanto ") to give it its proper grace. . .* Elsewhere he says : *When the Lady dances in a Fête, in counterpassing and retreating and in turning round to the one side or the other, she must never lift with her hand the train of her skirt or gown, unless she should find herself in a very restricted place. . .*

The galliard tunes are multifold. Arbeau begins by giving us his sample tune for the tourdion coupled with the ordinary cinq-pas, followed by a toe and heel passage. Next come two galliard tunes which he says were very popular formerly, (1) " La traditore my fa morire," (2) " Galliarde appellée Anthoinette." [2] After this he sets out a great number of variations on the cinq-pas, which form the ornate passages of which he speaks, setting them all to different

---

[1] I propose to use the Italian word " passeggio " to designate those sequences of steps which carry the dancer from one location to another, thus distinguishing it from the word " passage " used by Arbeau in connection with ornate variations of the cinq-pas of a stationary character.

[2] For these Arbeau indicates no steps.

tunes. After each of these passages he puts " Et ainsi continuant en répétant le commencement ".   This provokes a comment from Capriol, who says : *You command us to continue, repeating from the beginning.   By doing this one would only perform one kind of cinq-pas in a galliard.*

Arbeau : *That will be governed by the wish of the dancer ; for if he so likes, instead of repeating as he began he can produce a new sort of cinq-pas ; and it could but be a good thing that he should so do, provided that he always makes the counterpart of his set of cinq-pas* (left and right) : *and if the dancer finds himself pressed for room, so that he cannot go straight forward, he can dance the said cinq-pas in circular fashion and, in turning his body, try to find himself once more planted in front of the demoiselle.*

Capriol : *Must I dance my cinq-pas going straight ahead when the place allows of it ?*

Arbeau : *When I speak of going straight ahead, I mean not to turn the body entirely ; for you dance with a good grace when you turn now to the right side, now to the left towards the demoiselle, as though you would be fencing : for the right grève one should show the right side, and for the left grève, the left side.*

The first two galliard tunes, mentioned by Arbeau as having been well liked in former times, are the following :—

Air de la gaillarde appellée " La traditore my fa morire "

Air de la gaillarde appellée " Anthoinette "

It is put into the mouth of Capriol to announce his happy recollections of the galliard " Anthoinette " the which he recalls having seen danced in Orléans by his companions, himself being able both to sing the tune and to accompany it on the lute.

In view of the wide range of galliard tunes from which we may choose, I will set out, as performing examples, some personal favourites, fitting to each the appropriate variations suited to the music.

THE GALLIARD

Let it be here remarked that for dancing purposes one galliard bar comprises two triple time bars of music. In the two preceding galliard tunes and in all his other examples, Arbeau joins his two bars into one, eliminating the intervening bar line (although the time measure 3 stands at the beginning of the tune), in order to emphasize the close of each cadence.

THE EARL OF SALISBURY'S GALLIARD

" The Earl of Salisbury's Galliard " forms the sequel to the pavan of that name which has been set out in the preceding chapter, according to the plan of the first pavan contained in the Rawlinson manuscript. The galliard perforce contains the same number of strains and dancing-bars as its pavan.

The figures are as follows :—

First Strain : Double counterpassing with ordinary cinq-pas.

Repeat of First Strain : Cross-foot variation, followed by single counterpassing.

Second Strain : Over-foot variation, followed by single counterpassing.

Repeat of Second Strain : Side-crossed fleurets, followed by single counterpassing.

None of these composite variations are given distinguishing names by Arbeau, who merely details the successive movements. I therefore supply approximate translations from the Italian names, where they exist, and coin others where they are lacking.

The Steps : The cinq-pas in counterpassing should be performed as follows : Your path will be directed a little to the left and will describe a shallow curve. Stand with the right foot forward and on the first beat, hop on it, simultaneously kicking the left foot forward knee high, with straight knee and pointed toe. On the *half* of the beat, lower the left toe a few inches in advance of the right. This completes the left grève, which is the first step. On the second beat make the right grève in similar fashion. On the third beat make another left grève, and on the fourth beat, a right grève. Now comes the fifth step which is the cadence and occupies the last two beats, as follows : On the fifth beat press the toes of both feet on the ground and then jump high into the air (for a man) or moderately high (for a woman). As you jump, scoop the left foot forward and alight on both feet on the sixth beat, with the left foot forward in the fifth position. This is a left cadence.[1] For the counterpart go through the same sequence, beginning with the right foot, but this time you will be retreating, in this manner : Passing your partner on the left, make a half-turn right,[2]

[1] The dancer should alight on the toes, bending the knees outwards, afterwards straightening the knees and sinking the heels. When jumping he draws the hands inward and upward ; on alighting he spreads them downward and outward.

[2] This half-turn may be divided into two quarter-turns, the first at the beginning of the cadence and the second at the close.

at the close of the left cadence, so that you will again be facing one another with feet in the fifth position (right). Now hop on the left foot, on the first beat, and make the right grève ; but, on lowering the right foot, bring it down *behind* the left. On the second beat, hop on the right foot and make the left grève ; on lowering the left foot, bring it down behind the right. On the third and fourth beats, make the right and left grèves again in the same manner. On the fifth and sixth beats make the right cadence, scooping the foot forward, but bringing it down *behind* the left in the fifth position. In the first figure when you counterpass the second time, sustain the weight on the right foot and draw back the left toe in anticipation of the first beat, on the which you hop on the right foot and make left grève to start the second set of cinq-pas, counter-passing to your original positions.

Cross-foot Variation : On the first beat, hop on the *right* foot and cross the left foot over the right knee, lowering the left foot at the half-beat. Repeat this movement on the second beat. On the third beat, hop on the *left* foot and cross the right foot over the left knee, lowering the right foot at the half-beat. Repeat this movement on the fourth beat. On the fifth and sixth beats, make the left cadence, scooping the left foot forward as you jump and landing on both feet in the fifth position left. To complete the variation perform the same steps, using reverse feet, and concluding with the right cadence.

Over-foot Variation : Turn obliquely towards the left side, with the right foot forward. On the first beat, hop on the right foot, making simultaneously a left grève : at the half-beat, lower the left foot behind the right, so that the left toe almost touches the right heel. On the second beat, cross the right foot over the left, flat on the ground, with a little stamp, and at the half-beat, raising the left heel, stamp with the ball of the left foot. On the third beat, stamp again with the right foot and, with a right hop, raise the left foot backward. On the fourth beat, slip the toe of the left foot beneath the right heel, projecting the right foot forward in a grève [1] : at the half-beat, hop on the left foot, still holding the right raised in front. On the fifth beat, lower the right foot in front and perform the left cadence, landing on the sixth beat in the fifth position left. The counterpart of the variation is performed turning towards the right, using reverse feet and concluding with the right cadence.

The Side-crossed Fleurets : This ornate variation is performed rapidly, making one fleuret to a beat. On the first beat, hop sideways towards the left, on the left foot, and immediately cross the right foot over the left, treading only on the toes ; on the half-beat, make a left *entretaille* (i.e. slipping the left toe under the right heel) projecting the right foot forward in a *pied en l'air*. This constitutes a *left* side-crossed fleuret. On the second beat, make one to the *right*, on the third beat, another to the *left*, and on the fourth beat another to the *right*. On the fifth beat, lower the left foot (with which you will have made the last

[1] This is a left *entretaille*.

pied en l'air) behind the right, so that the toe is level with the right heel and perform the left cadence. The counterpart of the variation is performed, starting with the *right* side-crossed fleuret and concluding with the right cadence. This variation will be followed by the final counterpassing, after which the couple, meeting in the centre, will advance hand in hand to salute the company with a parting reverence. The man will then lead his partner back to her place, where they will make the " révérence salutatoire " towards each other.

Arm Movements : These should be gentle and natural, being the result of a slight turning of the body to right or left, leaving the arms on the other side. For instance, in making a left grève, it looks well to turn the head and shoulders a little toward the left, looking over at the left foot, and letting the hands lean towards the right, the same actions to be reversed when making a right grève. When making the cadence, draw the hands inwards and upwards while jumping, and downwards and outwards on alighting. As the feet touch the ground, bend the knees outwards ; then straighten them and lower the heels. This gives a spring to the step.

THE EARL OF SALISBURY'S GALLIARD
reduced to its rhythmic outline to demonstrate the sequences of steps

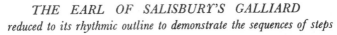

Passeggio of Cinq-pas l.r.l.r. Cadence.
Variation: Cross-foot l.l.r.r. Cadence.
Cinq-pas r.l.r.l. Cadence.
Cross-foot r.r.l.l. Cadence.

Passeggio: Cinq-pas l.r.l.r. Cadence.
Passeggio: Cinq-pas l.r.l.r. Cadence.
Cinq-pas r.l.r.l. Cadence.
Cinq-pas r.l.r.l. Cadence.

Variation: Over foot Cinq-pas, left.
Variation: Side-crossed Fleurets, left.
Over foot Cinq-pas, right.
Side-crossed Fleurets, right.

III

DANCES OF ENGLAND AND FRANCE

Passeggio: Cinq-pas **l. r. l. r.** Cadence. | Cinq-pas **r. l. r. l.** Cadence.
Passeggio: Cinq-pas **l. r. l. r.** Cadence. | Cinq-pas **r. l. r. l.** Cadence.

THE EARL OF SALISBURY'S GALLIARD

Wm. Byrd.

THE GALLIARD

Gagliarda la Tamburina

This very beautiful galliard tune is contained in a manuscript collection of sixteenth-century Italian, French, and English lute pieces, for many years the treasured possession of Arnold Dolmetsch, and now preserved in the Dolmetsch Library. The tune consists of six strains without repeats. In the opening bars of the first four strains the *bass*, which is divided into crotchets, gives the notes of the Indian *tambura*. The fourth strain has the unusual number of twelve bars instead of eight, making the equivalent of six dancing bars (or " galliard bars ") instead of four. The rhythmic flow of the music accords well with the light and fluent style of dancing, called by Arbeau " pas mignardés ". He says : *You will be making the pas mignardés when you extend the five minims into ten crotchets, and instead of making the whole step all at once with its little hop, you will make of it two parts. . . . And such pas mignardés are in truth but the cinq-pas, only they have a finer grace and are less heavy : for, instead of letting the body fall plumb in one go, one alights gradually* (car en lieu de tomber le corps à plomb d'un coup, on l'assied en trainant).[1]

The way in which one may lighten the *cinq-pas* in a galliard, as described by Arbeau, is at first difficult to elucidate until one realizes that the word *step* (" pas ") is used by him to indicate certain galliard movements such as " grève ",

---

[1] Spelling modernized.

" ruade ", " ru de vache ", etc., whereas the placing of the feet (" assiette des pieds ") is taken for granted and not referred to. When we bear this in mind his instructions become clear.

THE FIGURES OF GAGLIARDA LA TAMBURINA

First Strain : Single counterpassing with the *cinq-pas mignardés*, followed by the interlaced variation, termed by Caroso " i cinque passi intrecciati ".

Second Strain : Counterpassing with the *cinq-pas mignardés* followed by a revolving variation, termed by Caroso the " molinello " (little mill).

Third Strain : Counterpassing as before, followed by a heel and toe variation.

Fourth Strain : Counterpassing with *cinq-pas mignardés* followed by the *ruade-entretaille* variation. During the additional four bars (equal to two galliard bars) of this strain, the partners will again counterpass with the *cinq-pas mignardés*.

Fifth Strain : Variation, called by Caroso " campanelle " (little bells), followed by counterpassing as before.

Sixth Strain : Advance and retreat with hopped fleurets and receding fleurets (" recacciate "), followed by a passeggio composed of half steps in which the partners describe a *figure-eight* in opposite directions, meeting in the centre, and advancing towards the onlookers for the finale.

THE STEPS

The Cinq-pas Mignardés : Stand with the weight resting on the left foot and with the right foot forward. In slight anticipation of the first beat hop on the left foot and *exactly on* the beat step forward with the right : at the half-beat (sliding the left foot forward), make a left grève, turning the body a little towards the right side. Just before the second beat, hop on the right foot, and *exactly on* the beat step forward on the left : at the half-beat (sliding the right foot forward), make a right grève, turning the body obliquely to the left. For the third and fourth beats continue in the same manner, making alternately the left and right grève. During the fifth and sixth beats (after lowering the right foot), perform the left cadence, scooping the left foot forward and landing from the high jump in the fifth position left. As you alight, let the back foot touch the ground first to break the contact. Arbeau remarks that by this device one avoids falling like a sack of wheat (" car quand on les pose tous deux ensemblément, il semble que ce soit un sac de bled qui soit déchargé à terre "). Make the right counterpart in similar fashion, using reverse feet.

Interlaced Variation : This kind of cinq-pas is called by Caroso " i cinque passi intrecciati ", and should be performed as follows : Stand with the right foot forward and the weight resting thereon. On the first beat hop on it and simultaneously swing the left foot out sideways in a *ru de vache* (side-kick) :

at the half-beat lower it lightly to the ground crossed in front of the right and barely touching the ground. On the second beat, hop again on the right foot and swing the left out sideways in a second *ru de vache*, this time bringing the toe down across the back of the right heel, at the half-beat. Make two more left *ru de vache*, lowering the foot alternately across the toe and the heel of the right foot during the third and fourth beats. During the fifth and sixth beats, perform the left cadence. Make the right counterpart of this variation, using reverse feet.

The Molinello : This variation is performed revolving to the right for the first part (wherein the cinq-pas start with the left grève), and to the left for the counterpart, starting with the right grève. In the Molinello the steps can also be mignardés as follows : On the first beat, step with the right foot, spinning to the right, and at the half-beat, hop on it, making a left grève. On the second beat lower the left foot a few inches in front of the right and at the half-beat, hop on it, making a right backward kick (*ruade*). On the third beat, lower the right toe beneath the heel of the left foot in the manner of an entretaille ; and at the half-beat, hop on the right foot, projecting the left foot forward with a grève. On the fourth beat, lower the left foot in front of the right and at the half-beat, hop on it, making a right grève. On the fifth beat, lower the right foot and (pressing the feet on the ground to gain impetus), spring into the air, landing on the sixth beat. As you jump, scoop the left foot forward, but, as you alight, bring it down *behind* the right foot. This will enable you to make a quarter-turn left on the toes, so as to start revolving leftward for the counterpart. This is performed in the same manner as the first part, using reverse feet. The partners should arrange to be facing one another at the close of each cadence. The man may ornament his high jump by making a single or double turn in the air or by passing and counterpassing the feet.

Ruade Entretaille Variation: The steps to be employed are identical with those of the Molinello ; but, instead of revolving, the dancers remain facing each other throughout. The grace of this variation is greatly enhanced by appropriate arm movements which should be made as follows : For the first grève, draw the hands inward and upward, so that the fingertips meet at about chin-level. For the succeeding ruade, spread them downward and outward in a graceful curve ; for the next two grèves draw the hands toward the opposite side and look over at the raised foot. For the fifth and sixth beats, allotted to the cadence, make the same arm movements as those during the first and second beats. Lightly done, these balancing movements of head and arms lend much charm to this set of cinq-pas.

Campanelle Variation : This is done hopping on one foot and swinging the other back and forth like a bell clapper. For the left campanelle, make a quarter-turn to the right, so as to show the left side, but keep the head turned towards the partner. Turn the reverse way for the right campanelle. On the first beat, hop on the right foot and simultaneously draw back the left foot raised a few inches from the ground : at the half-beat hop again on the right foot and swing the left foot forward. This is one campanella. The movement is done only from the knee and the toe is not pointed. During the second, third, and fourth beats, make three more left campanelle. On the fifth beat lower the left foot and, scooping it forward, perform the left cadence, alighting on the sixth beat in the fifth position, but with the *left* foot *behind* the right. Make the right campanelle in similar fashion, turning obliquely leftward and concluding with the right cadence.

Hopped Fleurets : Stand on the right foot with the left foot forward, raised two inches from the ground. On the first beat, hop on the right foot, advancing a little as you do so ; then, quickly withdrawing the left foot, tap the toe lightly on the ground beside the right heel. At the half-beat, transfer the weight to the left foot by means of a jeté, springing on to the flat of the foot (which you bring forward, level with the right) ; *at the same time*, raise the right foot forward two inches from the ground. This constitutes a left fleuret. The right fleuret, made in similar fashion, follows on the second beat. Make another left fleuret on the third beat and another right fleuret on the fourth beat. On the fifth beat, lower the left foot so that the toe is level with the right heel and perform the left cadence, scooping the left foot forward as you jump and alighting on the sixth beat in the fifth position, with the left foot in front. During these fleurets the partners will have approached each other near the centre of the dance. The counterpart of this variation will consist of *recacciate* (backward hopped fleurets), by means of which the dancers retreat to their former positions.

Recacciate : Stand on the left foot with the right foot behind, raised two or three inches from the ground. On the first beat hop on the left foot, retreating a little as you do so ; then quickly tap the right toe on the ground behind the right heel. At the half-beat make a right *entretaille,* by slipping the right toe beneath the left heel. The left foot is thereby projected forward, but immediately drawn back behind the right, and raised two or three inches from the ground (with bent knee). This constitutes a right recacciata : make a left one on the second beat, a right one on the third beat, and a left one on the fourth beat. On the fifth beat, lower the right foot so that the toe is level with the left heel and perform the right cadence, landing on the sixth beat in the fifth position right.

Passeggio in Half-steps : These will be apportioned two to the crotchet (making four to the beat), and are done on the toes. The passeggio should describe a figure eight. The partners, who are facing each other at the start, begin by approaching the centre of the dance, turning obliquely towards the spectators ; then the lady circles to the left and the man to the right, each arriving half-way towards the centre at the end of the fourth beat. Here, during the fifth and sixth beats, they perform the left cadence face to face. For the counterpart they again approach the centre of the dance and then turning, the man to the left and the lady to the right, complete the circle at the end of the fourth beat. The man then takes his partner's left hand and they perform the right cadence, facing the spectators. It produces a pleasing effect if they can economize steps on their second circle so as to leave a few over, to trip towards the front hand in hand before the final cadence. These little half-steps should be made very lightly and springily with straightened knees.

Heel and Toe : First four beats, hop on right foot and touch ground alternately with left heel, extended sideways, and toe, in front of right foot : 5th and 6th beats, left cadence. Make counterpart with reverse feet.

GAGLIARDA TAMBURINA

Lute MS., Dolmetsch Library.

DANCES OF ENGLAND AND FRANCE

THE GALLIARD

GAILLARDE À LA LYONNAISE

Arbeau speaks of another manner of dancing the galliard, apparently of Southern origin, saying : *For some time past they dance the galliard in a fashion which they call La Lyonnaise, in which the dancer, making room for another, takes congé of the demoiselle, leaves her, and retires. She, thus left alone, continues the dance for a time, then goes and chooses another dancer, and, after they have danced together, she takes congé of him, and leaves him and retires ; and these changes continue as long as the galliard lasts.*

Capriol asks : *If there are not enough maidens or men for the changes, may one choose those who have already danced ?*

Arbeau replies : *You can do so. But this fashion was introduced so that all the demoiselles of the company might enter into the dance, in order to avoid the bad custom of some who, indiscreet in their affections, will always lead the favoured one : and also, by means of these exchanges, the less beautiful may be called to the dance.*

This diverting manner of dancing the galliard was called in Italy " Il Piantone " because, as Caroso explains, the dancer left his partner " planted " and she in turn did the same by his successor.

The Figures of the Dance : The couple which opens the dance should advance hand in hand, the lady being on the right of her partner, and after saluting the company, turn face to face for a formal reverence.

The First Strain : The man takes his partner's right hand in his own, raised shoulder-high, and together they revolve to the right with a wheeling motion, using one complete set of cinq-pas for the first half of the strain. When making the second cadence (right) the dancers should alight with the right foot drawn *back*, making fifth position *left*. This facilitates their making a half-turn right (changing the position to fifth position *right*), so as to perform the counter-revolution to the left, with left hands joined, during the second half.

Repeat of the First Strain : The partners separate. During the first half of the repeat the man performs a *campanelle* variation while the lady fills in with a passeggio of cinq-pas to left and right (keeping her face turned towards her partner) : in the second half she deftly executes a *toe and heel* variation, while the man makes the passeggio to left and right.

The Second Strain : Single counterpassing, followed by *underfoot* variation for both dancers.

Repeat of Strain : Single counterpassing, followed by *side-spring* variation for both dancers.

The Third Strain : Passage of onze-pas composed of ordinary fleurets, at the close of which the partners meet and make a parting reverence on the final chord. The man then retires.

Repeat of the Strain : The lady, dancing alone, advances towards the spectators with hopped fleurets, and retreats with recacciate. This occupies the first half of the repeat : during the second half she executes a graceful passeggio of half-steps on the toes, during which she goes to invite her new partner to the dance. During the final chord they salute each other with a formal reverence. This done, they advance hand in hand and the dance begins anew. This time it will be the lady who will retire after the close of the third strain, and the man who will dance, during the repeat, a variation followed by a passeggio in which he goes in quest of a new partner. This passeggio may consist of ordinary cinq-pas, or else of fleurets or of agile half-steps, according to his own preference. I have chosen the above figures and counterpassings of several kinds with a view to conveying the fullest information to the student concerning the diverse manners of dancing a galliard, so as to produce an effect of pleasing variety for the entertainment of the assembled company. I will next describe the manner of performing the above variations, and then suggest others that may be introduced by the succession of dancers.

How to Perform the Steps

The Cinq-pas in the Wheeling Movement : As the partners face each other after the opening reverence, the man takes the lady's right hand in his own and raises it shoulder-high.

Then proceed as follows :—

Standing with the weight on the right foot : On the first beat, hop on it and simultaneously raise the left foot forward, making a grève : at the half-beat, bring the left foot down a few inches in front of the right. On the second beat, hop on the left foot and make a right grève, lowering the foot at the half-beat. On the third beat, hop on the right foot and make a left grève : on the fourth beat, hop again on the left foot, making a right grève. On the fifth beat, start the left cadenza, pressing the toes of both feet on the ground to gain impetus for the high jump. Whilst executing the jump, scoop the left foot forward and before you alight on the sixth beat, draw it back again, so as to land in the fifth position right. This completes the first half of the cinq-pas : the counterpart is made in the same manner, using reverse feet, but still revolving to the right. For the second half of the strain make a rapid half-turn to the right and, holding left hands, perform the same figure, revolving to the left. At the close, release hands, with a courteous inclination.

The Campanelle Variation : This will be made exactly as described in the preceding dance, " Gagliarda la Tamburina." When making the left campanelle the man should turn his left side towards his partner, and the right side for the right campanelle. His face, however, is kept turned towards her. She meanwhile makes a passeggio in cinq-pas, of which the first half is made turned towards the left and the second half towards the right.

Toe and Heel Variation : This variation, which is called by Caroso " Punta e Calcagno ", differs from the " heel and toe " as described in " Gagliarda la Tamburina ", and should be performed as follows :—

Stand with the right foot forward and the weight resting on the left. On the first beat, drawing back the right foot so that the toe is level with the left heel, spring slightly towards the right, on to the right foot. Just after the beat, touch the ground with the point of the left toe in front of the right very lightly. On the second beat, hop on the right foot and touch the ground with the left heel, in front of the right toe, letting the left toe point upwards. On the third beat, spring towards the left on to the left foot, drawing it back so that the toe is level with the right heel, and just after the beat touch the ground with the right toe in front of the left. On the fourth beat, hop on the left foot and touch the ground with the right heel in front of the left toe. On the fifth beat, lower the right toe (which is pointing upwards) and, springing into the air, perform the left cadence, scooping the left foot forward as you jump, and landing on the sixth beat in the fifth position with the left foot forward (fifth position left). Perform the counterpart in the opposite sense with reverse feet.

Ruade-Entretaille Variation : This is performed as already explained in the directions for the " Gagliarda la Tamburina ", the steps being identical with those of the *molinello*, but performed facing forward in a stationary position and making the graceful arm movements which add to the charm of this variation.

Side-Crossed Fleurets : These are performed as explained in " The Earl of Salisbury's Galliard ".

Passage of Onze-pas, composed of ordinary fleurets : This figure of *onze-pas* occupies twelve beats instead of six for the half set and another twelve for the counterpart (four *galliard bars* in all). Each fleuret occupies two beats, so that five are made during ten beats and the last two beats are filled by the cadence.

Standing on the right foot with the left foot raised forward, rise on the toes and during the first beat make two half-steps in a light and springy manner (left and right) : on the second beat, step (toe first) on to the flat of the left foot, raising the right foot forward a few inches from the ground, neatly pointed. This constitutes a left ordinary fleuret. During the third and fourth beats make a right fleuret in similar fashion ; and so continue until you have made five fleurets, the last of which will be a left fleuret, which leaves you with the right foot raised forward. On the eleventh beat, lower it and perform the left cadence, scooping the left foot forward as you jump, but drawing it back again so as to land in the fifth position right forward. During the second half of the strain, make the counterpart, starting with a right fleuret and concluding with a right cadence. Make a reverence on the final chord.

The *hopped fleurets*, advancing, and *recacciate*, retreating, are as described in the instructions for the performance of " Gagliarda la Tamburina ".

Other figures may be chosen at pleasure, or the same figures repeated by succeeding dancers.

The two following will be found effective :—

(1) First beat, left posture ; second, left grève ; third (turning leftwards), right grève ; fourth, left grève ; fifth and sixth, right cadence : to be followed by the counterpart, using reverse feet and turning to the right. The posture consists in standing with weight on the back foot and delicately pointing the other forward in the fourth position. In *left posture* you point the left foot.

(2) First beat, draw back the forward foot into the first position (feet joined) ; second, right grève ; third, right ruade ; fourth, right entretaille causing left grève ; fifth and sixth, right cadence : to be followed by the counterpart. These being galliard movements will naturally be interspersed with hops in galliard fashion and, before making the cadenza, the foot which is raised should be lowered into the fifth position to gain impetus for the jump. If preferred, the cadence may be terminated in the fourth position (termed by Arbeau " posture "), instead of the fifth. This is quite good for the man, while the fifth position produces a neater effect for the lady.

GAILLARDE
(à la Lyonnaise)

Published by Pierre Attaignant. 1530.

122

THE FROG GALLIARD

This famous galliard, set by Thomas Morley, requires to go at a fairly quick pace. Consequently the cinq-pas in passeggio, passing and counterpassing, should be executed in simplified springing steps, instead of the composed hops employed in those galliards heretofore described. This deft springing from foot to foot, coupled with the bounding character of the music, produces a distinctly frog-like effect which is most diverting, when performed by a pair of agile dancers. For the intervening variations, some of the sets of abbreviated cinq-pas, termed by Arbeau " cinq-pas racoursis ",* will show to advantage taken at a quick tempo.

* I retain Arbeau's spelling.

Concerning these modified cinq-pas, which may be either reduced or multiplied, Arbeau says : *But you should take note that there are some cinq-pas which are called cinq-pas because they are measured by the same time measures as those of the cinq-pas : and nevertheless they contain either more or fewer than the five movements.*

" The Frog Galliard " contains two double length strains and their repeats. The figures selected for this galliard run as follows :—

First Strain : The dancers enter hand in hand (the lady on her partner's right) and advance up the centre, dancing the cinq-pas in springing steps. Arrived at the head of the dance, they separate and, describing a circular course, the lady turning right and the man left, they take up their station opposite to each other about six feet apart. This requires a double set of cinq-pas, and thus occupies half of the first strain. The second half will be filled by a stamping variation followed by a set of abbreviated cinq-pas which we will call " cinq-pas racourcis 1 " ; this brings us to the end of the strain.

Repeat of the First Strain : The couple counterpass with a double set of cinq-pas, describing a figure eight in their passeggio.

Second Half of the Strain : This is occupied by two stationary variations ; the first (which will be called " cinq-pas racoursis 2 ") is composed of *ru de vache*, second *ru de vache*, and *cadence*, followed by right counterpart. The second (" cinq-pas racoursis 3 ") is composed of two side-crossed fleurets and cadence, followed by right counterpart.

Second Strain, First Half : The couple counterpass with a double set of cinq-pas in a zig-zag movement, occupying half the strain.

Second Half of the Strain : This is occupied by two stationary variations of abbreviated cinq-pas (to be called " cinq-pas racoursis 4 and 5 "), which will be described in due course.

Repeat of Second Strain : The partners meet in the centre and, taking first right hands and then left, revolve to right and left, finally returning to their original places. This takes a double set of cinq-pas in passeggio, occupying half the strain.

Second Half of the Strain : The couple execute a passeggio composed of scurrying half-steps wherein the man pursues his partner and catches up with her for the last quarter of the strain, in which they advance with the same half-steps towards the audience till they reach the head of the dance, when they perform a high jump on the final chord. This makes an effective conclusion to a charming galliard.

How to Perform the Steps

Simplified Cinq-pas in Passeggio : Stand on the right foot with the left foot forward and raised a few inches from the ground. On the first beat, spring lightly on to the left foot, simultaneously raising the right foot forward in a *grève* :

on the second beat, spring on to the right foot, making a left grève : on the third beat, spring again on to the left foot, making a right grève. On the fourth beat, lower the right foot in front of the left in the fifth position, bending the knees slightly outwards : on the fifth and sixth beats, perform the left cadence, jumping high into the air, simultaneously scooping the left foot forward. As you descend, draw it back again so as to land, on the sixth beat, in the fifth position right forward. Perform the counterpart in similar fashion, using reverse feet and concluding with a right cadence. Continue with a second set of the same cinq-pas which brings you half-way through the strain, ready for the first variation.

First Variation : This is the stamping figure. Turn obliquely towards the right and on the first beat, hop on the right foot simultaneously crossing the left foot over the right knee. On the second beat stamp with the left foot in front of the right in the fifth position, and follow this at the *half*-beat, by stamping with the right toe behind the left heel. On the third beat, stamp again with the flat of the left foot in front of the right ; on the fourth beat, make an entretaille with the right foot beneath the left heel : on the fifth beat, make a high jump, throwing the left foot forward and drawing it back rapidly : on the sixth beat land in the fifth position (right foot forward), bending the knees outwards and straightening them at the half-beat. Make the counterpart in similar fashion, using reverse feet. This quick stamping, left and right, requires small movements.

Cinq-pas Racoursis 1 : On the first beat make a left grève ; on the second beat draw it back into a *ruade*, trailing it along the ground as you do so : on the third beat make a left entretaille, projecting the right foot forward in a grève : on the fourth beat, lower the right foot in front of the left in the fifth position, bending the knees outwards : on the fifth beat, make a high jump, throwing the left foot forward and drawing it back rapidly : on the sixth beat, land in the fifth position (right foot forward), bending the knees outwards and straightening them at the half-beat. Make the counterpart, using reverse feet.

In the counterpassing figure that follows, making the pattern of a figure eight, the lady circles to her right and the man to his left ; they then pass one another, each keeping to the left. On arriving at the end of the course, the lady circles to her left and the man to his right ; at the close of the half-strain, they take up their station facing each other as before, six feet apart, but on opposite sides from where they started.

Cinq-pas Racoursis 2 : On the first beat, hop on the left foot and simultaneously fling the right foot out sideways in a *ru de vache :* on the second beat, without hopping, bring the right toe down lightly in front of the left foot ; on the third beat hop again on the left foot and make a second *ru de vache* with the right : on the fourth beat, without hopping, bring the right toe down lightly behind the left heel and bend both knees : on the fifth beat make a high jump, throwing the left foot forward and drawing it back again so as to land on the sixth beat in the fifth position right. If you have sufficient agility you may pass the left foot forward and back a second time. Complete the set with the counterpart, using reverse feet.

Cinq-pas Racoursis 3 : This consists of two sidecrossed fleurets and cadence. On the first beat make a sideways spring on to the right toe and then bring the left toe down across the front of the right, transferring the weight on to the left toe : on the second beat, drawing the right foot rapidly back, make an *entretaille* beneath the left heel projecting the left foot forward. (This is one sidecrossed fleuret.) On the third beat, spring sideways on the the left toe and bring the right toe down across the left foot, transferring the weight on to the right toe : on the fourth beat, drawing back the left foot, make a right *entretaille*, projecting the right foot forward (this completes the second sidecrossed fleuret) : on the fifth beat bring the right foot down level with the left in the first position and perform the left cadence, scooping the left forward as you jump and drawing it back again so as to land on the sixth beat in the fifth position right. Complete the set with the counterpart, using reverse feet. In the *counterpassing figure* that follows, pursue a zigzag course, the one advancing obliquely as the other goes towards the back of the stage or room. The same single springing steps are used as in the preceding passeggii. In the previous counterpassing the partners have already changed sides ; so now the lady will make one half-set of cinq-pas advancing obliquely towards the right, whereas the man turns a little away from the audience and goes obliquely towards the back stage. For the counterpart they reverse direction, the man coming forward and the lady going back. By this time, the partners should be half-way across. A second complete set of cinq-pas is made in the same manner so that the partners will have changed places and will turn to face one another (with a quarter-turn right) for the final cadence. This completes the first half of the second strain.

Cinq-pas Racoursis 4 : Stand on the right foot with the left foot advanced without any weight on it. On the first beat, draw the left foot back a few inches behind the right in the fourth position, bending both knees : on the second beat, transfer the weight on to the left foot and straighten the right knee, drawing the hands gracefully backwards towards the left. This is a half reverence (révérence passagère). On the third beat, hop on the left foot and cross the right in front of the left knee : on the fourth beat bring the right foot down in front of the left, in the fifth position. On the fifth beat perform the left cadence by jumping high into the air and revolving to the right. Scoop the left foot forward as you jump and draw it back again, landing on the sixth beat, opposite your partner, with the right foot forward in the fifth position. Throw the weight on to the left foot so as to be ready for the right counterpart, which brings you to the end of the strain.

THE GALLIARD

Cinq-pas Racoursis 5 : Stand on the right foot with the left foot advanced without any weight on it. On the first beat, hop on the right foot and cross the left foot over the right knee : on the second beat, lower the left foot and slide it backwards briskly, making a *ruade :* on the third beat, make a left *entretaille,* projecting the right foot forward in a *grève :* on the fourth beat, lower the right foot in front of the left in the fifth position, bending both knees. On the fifth beat, make a high jump, passing and repassing the feet : land on the sixth beat with the right foot forward in the fifth position, bending the knees outwards and straightening them again. Perform the counterpart in similar fashion, using reverse feet. This completes the second strain.

The Revolving Passeggio : This occupies one-half of the repeat of the second strain, and takes two sets of cinq-pas. The first half-set brings the partners together and its counterpart is used for the revolution to the right, holding right hands, shoulder-high. The second half-set makes the revolution to the left and its counterpart takes them on a circular course back to their original places. For this the lady turns to the right and the man to the left. They face each other for the final cadence. The same springing steps are used in this passeggio as in the others.

The Finale, composed of Scurrying Half-steps : These should be executed with agility in a light springy way on the toes with straightened knees. To begin with, the lady may make a turning movement to the right, then cross the stage or room and loop back again, finally allowing herself to be overtaken at the foot of the dance in the centre. Here the man passes behind her, and, taking her left hand in his right, leads her forward to the head of the dance where they greet the spectators with a final high jump, followed by a parting reverence on the concluding chord. Two half-steps go to a beat.

THE FROG GALLIARD

Thomas Morley.

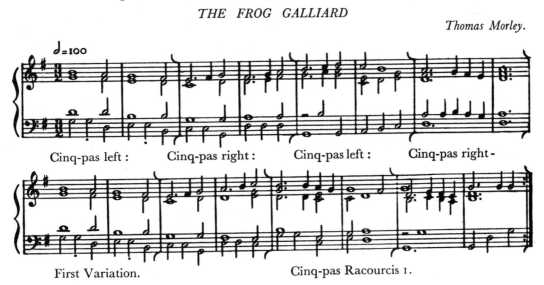

Cinq-pas left : Cinq-pas right : Cinq-pas left : Cinq-pas right-

First Variation. Cinq-pas Racourcis 1.

Galliards.

Stanza 67   But for more divers and more pleasing show,
                  A swift and wand'ring dance he did invent,
                  With passages uncertain, to and fro,
                  Yet with a certain answer and consent
                  To the quick music of the instrument.
                  Five was the number of the music's feet,
                  Which still the dance did with five paces meet.

Stanza 68   A gallant dance, that lively doth bewray
                  A spirit and a virtue masculine,
                  Impatient that her house on earth should stay,
                  Since she herself is fiery and divine.
                  Oft doth she make her body upward flyne
                  With lofty turns and caprioles in the air,
                  Which with the lusty tunes accordeth fair.

                     (Orchestra)

Queen Elizabeth dancing La Volta with the Earl of Leicester.

Painting at Penshurst Place, Kent.

By kind permission of Lord De L'Isle and Dudley.

[face p. 128

CHAPTER VII

LA VOLTA AND THE CORANTO

LA VOLTA

IT is surprising that concerning this once popular dance, made familiar to us in literature and connected historically with Queen Elizabeth, no technical description would have reached us were it not for our admirable teacher Arbeau, to whom we are deeply indebted. There is indeed a dance described by Cesare Negri [1] under the name of " La Nizzarda " (a dance of Nice), which is obviously a version of the volte ; but, had we not learned from Arbeau how, technically, to execute the volte, we would most probably not have seen the connection. In the previously cited " Arnold Dolmetsch Lute Manuscript " (c. 1610), there occurs not only a volte tambourina,[2] following on the galliard of that name, but a succession of twenty-six other voltes. We may deduce therefrom that this famous dance excited at the close of the sixteenth century a strong, though short-lived enthusiasm. I will proceed with a literal translation of Arbeau's instructions, adding thereto the result of my own practical experience in the most convenient and effective manner of performing this dance.

La Volte

The volte is a species of galliard familiar to the Provenceaux, the which is danced like the tourdion in triple time (" mesure ternaire ") : the movements and steps of this dance are made in turning the body, and consist of two steps, a rest for the high jump, a placing of the joined feet and two rests or pauses. In order to understand this, imagine yourself facing me with joined feet, make for the first step a " pied en l'air ",[3] rather short, while hopping on your left foot, and while doing this, you will show me your left shoulder, then make the second step fairly long on your right foot without hopping and in doing this show me your back. Then make the high jump turning your body and alight on joined feet, in doing which you will show me your right shoulder : thus you will have accomplished the first turn.

Capriol : *On your showing, one does not completely turn the body.*

Arbeau : *He who would make an entire turning of the body, would find himself as at the beginning, and would scarcely alter his position : after this first turn (which is*

---

[1] Inventione di Balli.

[2] So spelt in the MS. the which seems to be the work of a French scribe.

[3] Arbeau omits to point out that the *pied en l'air* is made with the right foot whilst hopping on the left.

a three-quarter turn of the body), you will make at the second turn a fairly short pied en l'air as before, hopping on the left foot, and in doing this you will show me your stomach : then you will make the second step fairly long on your right foot without hopping, and in doing this you will show me your left shoulder : then you will make the high jump, turning your body, and will alight on your joined feet, which doing you will show me your back.

For the third turn and cadence, you will make a pied en l'air for the first step, rather short, hopping on your left foot, and in doing this will show me your right side. Then you will make the second step fairly long on your right foot without hopping, in doing which you will show me your stomach : then you will make the high jump, turning your body, and will alight on joined feet, which doing you will show me your left shoulder.

For the fourth turn and cadence, you will make a pied en l'air for the first step rather short, hopping on your left foot, and in doing this you will show me your back : then you will make the second step fairly long on the right foot without hopping, in doing which you will show me your right shoulder : then you will make the high jump turning your body, and will alight on joined feet, which doing you will show me your stomach, as you were placed at the beginning : it is not always a necessity to do exactly as I prescribe, for it might happen that you would turn more or less quickly : but I have made you this hypothesis for the sake of clarity.

Capriol : If I hold a demoiselle by the hand, it would be impossible for her to make the turn with me, the more so as she would be farther from the centre.

Arbeau : Your argument is good, supposing (as it is true) that the demoiselle makes the same steps and movements as yourself : and for this occasion he who dances the volte contemplating himself as the centre and middle of a circle, should draw the demoiselle as close as possible to his own body when he wishes to turn, for by this means the said demoiselle will find the steps less widely spaced and easier to make : to draw her close to you do as follows : After you have made your reverence (holding the demoiselle by the hand) before making the revolutions, circle the room for a little, as a kind of preparation, as though you were dancing the tourdion : here take note that some people dance this commencement in cinq-pas right and cinq-pas left alternately, or else as cinq-pas racoursis in two steps, a high jump and a posture and the same for the counterpart and so continuing : others dance this commencement as with the rest of the volte by one pied en l'air, one step, a high jump, and the posture with joined feet as has been explained above.

Capriol : Which kind pleases you the most ?

Arbeau : The last kind. For in this manner the dance remains uniform in all its parts, as much in the beginning as at the end. When you wish to revolve, let go of the lady's left hand and place your left arm on her back, taking her and, holding her tight with your left hand, by the waist above the right hip,[1] and at the same instant you will place your right hand beneath her busk to help her to jump when you will push her before you with your left thigh. She for her part will put her right hand on your back or your collar, and will place her left hand against her thigh to hold down her skirt or her robe, lest in gathering the wind it should display her chemise or her bare leg : this done you will

[1] It is the *arm* that is over the right hip, the *hand* being nearer to the left hip.

130

go on making the revolutions of the volte, as explained above : and after having turned by as many cadences as you please, restore the demoiselle to her place where she will feel (no matter what good countenance she makes) her head whirling, full of vertigo and giddiness, and you perhaps will be much the same : I leave you to judge whether it be a proper thing for a young girl to make large steps and wide movements of the legs : and whether in this volte her honour and well-being are not risked and involved. I have already told you my opinion.

Capriol : *This vertigo and giddiness would distress me.*

Arbeau : *Then dance some other kind of dance. Or if you dance this one, leftwards, begin again to dance it once more to the right, and thus you will unturn the second time that which you have turned the first.*

Here follows a nondescript tune in the rhythm of the volte, with beside it the steps in detail : First beat, *small step hopping on the left to make a right pied en l'air* : second beat, *larger step with the right* : third beat, *high jump followed by posture with joined feet* (pause). This formula is repeated throughout the tune. Arbeau then concludes by explaining how when the couple wish to dance the volte to the right all the manœuvres must be reversed and opposite feet used. He emphasizes the quickness and adroitness that must be used by the man in seizing his partner, swinging her into juxtaposition, grasping her tightly and throwing her up into the air (she practically sitting on his knee for this operation). This part of the volte is admirably illustrated in the picture in Penshurst Place, wherein the central figures are said to be Queen Elizabeth dancing with the Earl of Leicester.

Round about are other figures hand in hand modestly circling the room. In practice, I have found that the best way to dance the volte with impunity is to alternate the turning movement with the passeggio and later on to perform the whole, anti-clockwise. If the movements of both dancers are well synchronized in the revolving movement, the lady may rise to surprising heights. One point which Arbeau fails to make clear is that when throwing his partner up, it is impossible for the man to jump also (neither does he do so in " La Nizzarda "). He must content himself with a turning movement on the toes and reserve his high jumps for the passeggio, whilst in the revolving part, as the lady prepares her upward spring, he must raise his knee so as to project her. Since ladies nowadays do not wear stiff busks, the man is deprived of this assistance and can merely place his hand firmly across her middle ; she, however, being freer in her movements without the stiff, compressing busk, can spring more vigorously and will do well to place her hand on her partner's shoulder, rather than on his collar, thereby gaining in impetus. The man must beware of turning too sharply, lest he throw the lady off her balance ; and she for her part must remain completely upright and be careful not to poke her head forward. As she alights on the fourth beat, she must bend both knees outwards then rise on the toes and descend on to the flat of the feet at the sixth beat.

DANCES OF ENGLAND AND FRANCE

This adds grace and springiness to the conclusion of the cadence. It will be observed that, as in the galliard proper, two musical bars of triple time form one bar of the dance.

It is important that the dancers should realize that in the first passeggio, wherein the dancers hop on the left foot, making right grève, followed by right forward step and high jump (cadence), the man holds his partner's left hand in his right hand as they circle the room clockwise (i.e. the way of the sun). When the transition is made to the revolving movement, the man swings his partner swiftly round to his left side, grasps her waist with his left hand and her middle with his right hand : he thus pivots to the *right*, while she forms the outside of the wheel.

When Arbeau speaks of dancing the volte leftwards and afterwards to the right, he is alluding to the steps, which start with left hop in the opening, or with right hop for the reverse movement to counteract giddiness.

The most beautiful and inspiring volte that I know is by William Byrd ; so I choose that for a good practical example for those who would perform this dance.

LA VOLTA

William Byrd.

Hopped grève: step: jump: alight.

LA VOLTA AND THE CORANTO

THE COURANTE

Concerning the sixteenth-century courante, Thomas Morley says : " Like unto this " (viz. the branle double, by which he means the branle de Poitou in triple time), " but more light, be the voltes and courantes, which being both of a measure are notwithstanding danced after sundry fashions, the volte rising and leaping, the courante travising and running." All courantes (usually termed *coranto* in England) are in triple time and it is therefore surprising to discover that Arbeau writes his example in duple time. As, however, he states that the courante is in " mesure binaire legière ", I conclude that he intends the accented beat to be twice the length of the other. Since the steps of the courante fall only on the accented beats, this would in effect amount to quick triple time and be taken as such by the dancer. As Arbeau gives them they are delightfully simple and light, producing the effect of a sprightly skipping motion. The contemporary example of the courante (" Corriente ") given by Cesare Negri will be included in the Spanish-Italian volume of this work.

The steps, described by Arbeau, run on the formal pattern of two singles and a double, as with the pavan. These, however, are performed with light hops and springs which lend to this dance an airy grace in strong contrast to the solemn pavan although, basically, the steps are the same. Arbeau remarks : *It* (the courante) *differs considerably from the volte and is danced in light duple time, either advancing or sideways ; and sometimes retreating, according to the dancer's pleasure : and you will note that you must hop the steps of the courante, which is not done in the pavan, nor in the basse dance : to make then a left single, you, who are in comely posture* (" contenance décente ", i.e. with feet joined in the first position), *will hop on the right foot, putting down the left, for your first step. Then you will jump on to the right foot, landing with joined feet* (first position) *for the second step ; and thus will be accomplished the left single : the same you will make in reverse fashion, in order to accomplish the right single : for the left double, you will hop on the right foot, putting down the left foot for the first step of the said left double : then you will hop on the left foot, making the second step with the right foot ; then you will hop on the right foot, making the third step with the left foot : then you will jump on to the right foot, making the fourth step with joined feet* (first position) : *and thus will be accomplished the left double : the same you will do in reverse fashion for the two right singles and the double.* (When Arbeau speaks of two right or left singles he means that the *first* of the pair is right or left.)

Here some explanation will be helpful : to execute the left single rhythmically, you must make the preliminary hop with the right foot in anticipation of the beat and step with the left foot exactly on the beat : to complete the left single, join the right foot to the left (at the second bar) with a spring, landing in the first position. The right single should be performed the same way, by using reverse feet. For the left double, hop on the right foot in anticipation of the first beat (i.e. *bar*), and step with the left exactly on the beat. Just before the second beat (or bar), hop on the left foot and step with the right exactly on the beat. Make the third step as the first and the fourth by joining the right foot to the left, with a spring, landing (at the fourth bar) in the first position. Make the right doubles in the same way, using reverse feet. One movement goes to a bar of quick triple time, so that each *single* occupies two bars and each double four. When we speak of a " beat " with the courante, therefore, it is the accented beat that is implied.

The English usually called the courante *coranto* or *corranto*, and sometimes *corant* and *currant*. An effective way of performing the accompanying little English coranto is as follows : Let the couple advance hand in hand with two singles (left and right) and a double, hopped in the manner described above. Then let them retreat with right and left single and advance again with right double. Here they release hands and turn to face one another. They proceed with the same series of movements but danced sideways as in the branles, thus going in contrary motion. This brings us to the coda of the tune and here the couple join hands once more and advance towards the onlookers with left and right single, retreating with left double. Again they advance with right and left singles and continue to advance with the right double, at the conclusion of which they graciously salute the company with a parting reverence, performed with airy lightness, on the final chord.

ENGLISH CORRANTO

Anon., sixteenth century.

134

Arbeau picturesquely describes the early sixteenth century courante, treated as a mimed ballet, saying : *In my young days they made of the courante a kind of play and ballet : for three young men chose three young girls : and, having placed themselves in a row, the first dancer with his demoiselle then led her to a position at the other end of the room, and returned alone to rejoin his companions : the second then did the same, then the third, so that the three girls remained apart at one end of the room, and the three young men at the other : and when the third (young man) had returned, the first went frolicking and making several amorous overtures and gestures, such as dusting and pulling up his hose and arranging his chemise becomingly, whilst going in quest of his demoiselle, who for her part refused him her hand, or turned her back upon him, seeing which, the young man returned to his place with an appearance of despair : the two others went through the same performance. Finally they went all three together in quest of the said demoiselles, each one for his own, going down on one knee, and begging for mercy with joined hands : then the said demoiselles surrendered themselves into their arms and danced the said courante pell mell.*

Arbeau goes on to speak of the degeneration that has overtaken the courante, in later times, the young men having become careless and inexact in their steps. He asserts that they *dance according to their fancy and are content provided that they fall in cadence, and in dancing they turn their bodies, letting go of the demoiselle's hand ; and after that the revolution is accomplished, still dancing, they again take the hand of the demoiselle and continue the dance : and when the companions of him who dances see that he has become tired, they come and take away and steal from him his demoiselle and lead her to the dance or else he takes up with another partner, when he perceives that the first one is fatigued.*

After giving us a tune in duple time (somewhat suggestive of a branle), together with its tablature, Arbeau explains that the intervening (i.e. unaccented) notes are to be filled in by the hops and that when the dancer shall have become very tired, he may omit the hops, letting the said intervening notes serve as rests. Thus it appears that much freedom is permissible with the courante whose steps may serve as a basis for either of the foregoing types of dance or some other fanciful form.

SIR JOHN HOPE'S CURRANT

Set by Arnold Dolmetsch.

Anon., sixteenth century.

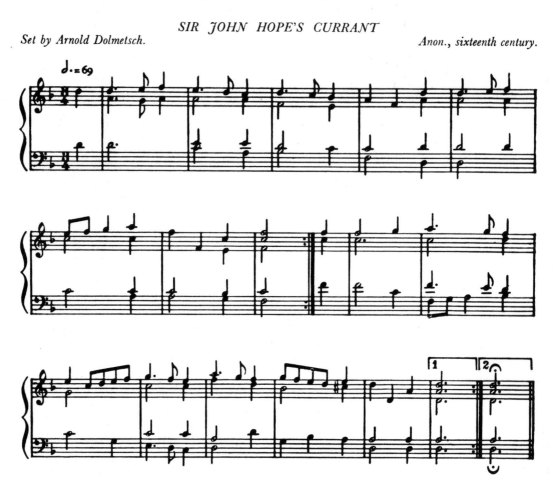

The Bodleian Library manuscript from which we have learned how to dance " My Lord of Essex Measure " (MS. Rawl., Poet 108), also enumerates the steps and evolutions proper to the *Coranto d'Espagne*, here entitled " Coranto Dyspyne ". This example is of considerable length ; but, when set to an appropriate tune, should be easily memorized, as the arrangement of the various movements is systematic. The title given to this dance suggests the idea that the courante anciently came from Spain, since it was a common practice to connect the name of a popular dance with that of its district, or country of origin. This supposition is further strengthened by the fact that Cesare Negri, who had his school of dancing in Milan from 1550 to the close of the sixteenth century, names his example " Corriente ", not " Coranto ".

Milan at that time was a Spanish possession and Negri gives us several other Spanish dances of great interest and beauty.

I will now set forth the directions for the Coranto d'Espagne, only modernizing the spelling and punctuating and classifying the steps to make them easily intelligible.

CORANTO D'ESPAGNE

List of Steps

First Time of Tune.

(1) *4 singles sideways, 2 singles and a double forward* (16 bars = first strain once)'

(2) *2 singles sideways, a reprise backwards twice* (16 bars = repeat of first strain).

(3) *4 singles sideways, a double forward, reprise backward* (16 bars = second strain).

In the MS. the word *twice* occurs at the close of the third section.

(4) Repeat this section therefore (16 bars = repeat of second strain).

Second Time of Tune.

(1) *4 singles sideways, a double forward, reprise backwards* (16 bars = first strain).

In the MS. the word *twice* occurs at the close of the preceding section.

(2) Repeat this section therefore (16 bars = repeat of first strain).

(3) *2 singles sideways, 3 treads forward ; 2 singles sideways, 3 treads backward* (16 bars = second strain).

(4) *A double forward, reprise backward twice* (16 bars = repeat of second strain).

Third Time of Tune.

(1) *2 singles sideways, 3 treads forward ; 2 singles sideways, 3 treads backward* (16 bars = first strain).

(2) *A double forward, reprise backward twice* (16 bars = repeat of first strain).

(3) *A double round both ways : one single backward and honour, a double into each other's place* (16 bars = second strain).

(4) *And let the women lead a double forward, reprise backward twice* (16 bars = repeat of second strain).

Fourth Time of Tune.

(1) *A double forward both ways* (i.e. left and right), *one single backward and honour, a double into your own places* (16 bars = first strain).

(2) *Lead a double forward* (i.e. partners holding hands), *reprise backward twice* (16 bars = repeat of first strain).

(3) *One single backward and honour, a double forward, reprise backward, one single backward and honour* (16 bars = second strain).

(4) Repeat this section (16 bars = repeat of second strain).

Fifth Time of Tune.

(1) Part : *4 doubles to and fro between your women* (16 bars = first strain).

(2) *And when you be all past them, then come sidelong to them with 3 treads, and honours* (16 bars, allowing for three couples to get back into position = repeat of first strain).

(3) The same as section (1), but this time it is specified that the first double is made forward. This facilitates the working of the interlacing figure in the opposite direction. The first time having been started from behind the row of women (16 bars = second strain).

(4) The same as section (2) (16 bars = repeat of second strain).

Finale : Tune straight through without repeats.

(1) *Then let the women lead a double forward reprise backward twice* (16 bars = first strain).

(2) *One single backward and honour, lead out* (16 bars = second strain).

This finale appears incomplete, as though there were some accidental omission. If it is desired to have the tune played with its repeats, as with the preceding figures, two other sections could be interpolated. The following arrangement would make a well-balanced conclusion, in place of the above incomplete finale.

(1) Let the women lead a double forward and reprise backward twice (16 bars = first strain).

(2) 4 singles sideways, a double forward, and reprise backward (16 bars = repeat of first strain).

(3) Lead a double forward (partners holding hands), and reprise backward twice (16 bars = second strain).

(4) One single backward and honour.

Lead [1] out (16 bars = repeat of second strain).

---

[1] In the manuscript on two occasions the figure of a hand is substituted for the word " lead ". This is to indicate that the partners go hand in hand.

LA VOLTA AND THE CORANTO

THE FIGURES OF THE DANCE

This coranto should be danced by three couples who, having entered in pairs, range themselves in a row facing the onlookers. Each man stands on the left of his partner, holding her left hand in his own right. The left hand, outside couple, from the dancers' standpoint, counts as the first couple. On the preliminary chord the dancers make a saluting reverence towards the company. The partners then turn to face each other for the four sideways singles, each moving alternately to left and right, so that they go in opposite directions. After the four sideways singles they turn again to face the onlookers for the two doubles forward. In the second section they face each other for the sideways singles and face front again for the reprise. In the third and fourth sections they face each other for the sideways singles and face front again for the ensuing double and reprise.

FIGURE II

In the first two sections the movements are similar to those of the third and fourth sections of Figure I. In sections 3 and 4 the dancers face front throughout, including the pair of singles in which they hop first to the left and then to the right, reversing the direction in the repeat.

FIGURE III

In the first two sections they continue to face forward. In section 3 the partners face each other for the two doubles round, during the first of which (a left double) the man takes his partner's right hand in his own and they revolve to the right : for the second (which is the right double), he takes her left hand in his own and they revolve to the left, returning to their respective positions. Now they perform the backward single and honour (which amounts to a saluting reverence), the man holding his partner's right hand in his own and then pass leftwards into each other's places.

In section 4 they release hands and the men stand still facing front while the women, likewise facing front, make a double forward and reprise backward twice, starting with the left foot the first time and the right foot the second time.

FIGURE IV

Section 1 : The men hold their partner's *right* hand in their own *left* and they make two doubles forward (*l.* and *r.*) ; they then turn to face each other for the left single backward and honour, each man taking his partner's right hand in his own. Then, making a left double, they return to their original places, passing to their left. At the close they should turn to face the spectators.

Section 2 : Each man holding his partner's left hand, they proceed with the alternated doubles and reprises.

Sections 3 and 4 : For the backward singles and honour, partners face each other but during the double and reprise all face forward.

Figure V

This is the interlacing figure whose twining movement was called in England *the hay* or *hey*. This characteristic term was borrowed from the French " La Haye ", likening the movement of the dancers to an artificial hedge, composed of upright stakes interlaced with horizontal stems or branches.

Section 1 : The couples separate, the women remaining in their places while the men, turning from them towards back stage with a half-turn left, start the first double with the left foot. The first man follows a circular path to the right, passing round and in front of the first woman and between her and the second woman. With the second double (beginning right foot), he passes behind the second woman and between her and the third woman. With the third double he passes in front of the third woman and round her right side as though there were another woman beyond her. With the fourth double he passes as though behind the imaginary fourth woman and, circling leftwards, arrives opposite the third woman but several paces distant. Then following a convex path he makes his three sideways treads, coming to rest in front of the first woman where he stands until his two followers have arrived in front of their respective partners. When all are in place they conclude with a backward single and honour. The second man (while the first is making his first double), turning towards back stage, performs a left double behind the row, pursuing a circular course so as to arrive beside the first woman in time to begin his second double. With the second double he passes in front of her and between her and the second woman. With his third double he passes behind the second woman and between her and the third woman. With his fourth double he passes in front of the third woman and along her right side as though there were a fourth woman beyond her. This concludes his part in the hay ; but he must now make a fifth double describing a circular course leftwards as did the first man. He requires, however, to make a longer loop so as to arrive a little beyond the row of women, from which position he can so arrange his three sideways treads as to come to a halt in front of the second woman, where he will stand still until the third man arrives. The third man, who will also have made a half turn left (turning his back on the audience), makes his first double to the right behind the row describing a shallow curve, then, with a second double, follows in the wake of the second man, so as to arrive beside the first woman in time for the third double. With his third double he passes in front of her and between her and the second woman. With his fourth double he passes behind the second woman and between her and the third woman. Then, making a fifth double, he passes in front of her and round her right side. With a sixth double he circles to the left, making a yet larger loop than his predecessors, so as to have a sufficient course in which to perform his three sideways treads in a convex curve, arriving at the close opposite to the third woman his own partner.

All being now in a row opposite to their respective partners, each man takes the right hand of his own and, making a quarter-turn left, on the toe of his left foot, performs a right backward single, bending the knees and bowing the head. The woman performs the same action, making a quarter-turn left on her left toe simultaneously with his, so that they come into line, face to face and side view to the spectators. It will be seen from the above directions that the *four* doubles prescribed in the list of steps apply only to the first man as he makes the haye. The second and third man following up behind make five and six doubles respectively, four of which belong to the hay.

Sections 3 and 4 form the counterpart of 1 and 2 of this figure. In the counterpart the hay starts from the other end with the third man and instead of beginning behind the row of women it starts from the front with a forward double. The third man, who now becomes the leader, circles round to the right and passes behind the third woman, in front of the second and behind the first, the others following in his wake. They make their loop at the end round an imaginary fourth person and then sidle along to the left till they arrive opposite to their partners. When they are all in position they make the right backward single and honour as before, falling back into line.

FIGURE VI

In sections 1 and 3 the row of dancers will face forward, each man holding his partner's left hand in his right.

In section 2 the partners turn to face each other for the sideways singles and turn frontways for the double and reprise.

In section 4 the partners, turning obliquely towards each other, make the backward single and honour, using the left foot. This occupies *four* bars, and during the succeeding four bars they salute the company in similar fashion again using the left foot. They then dance out in pairs with two singles and a double, the first couple leading.

How to Perform the Steps

The Forward Singles and Doubles : These will be performed as described in the French coranto, each step being anticipated by a hop on the other foot, and the joining of the feet at the close effected by means of a little spring landing on the final beat with feet joined in the first position.

The Sideways Singles : These also are the same as in the French coranto.

The Reprise : This retreating movement in the coranto is merely a backward hopped double, made gracefully turning the body to left and right whilst stepping backwards, at the same time raising the other foot forward well pointed.

The Forward Treads : The left forward tread is made stepping forward on the flat of the left foot without hopping and immediately rising on the toe. This takes one bar. On the second bar, step forward on the flat of the right foot and rise on the toe. On the third bar, step again on the flat of the left foot and rise on the toe. On the fourth bar, sink the heels, remaining stationary in the fourth position left. This sequence of three treads, in a light dance, corresponds with the Italian " seguito ordinario " ; used in a slow dance they would be done more smoothly and called a " seguito grave ".

The Backward Treads : These occur in this coranto when retreating after the second pair of sideways singles, so will begin with the right foot. Step back on the flat of the right foot and point the left toe in front of the right. On the second bar step back with the left foot similarly and on the third bar step back again with the right. On the fourth bar sink the left heel, remaining with the feet in the fourth position left.

The Sideways Treads : These move to the right in section 2 and to the left in section 4. On the first bar (right treads), step sideways on the flat of the right foot and draw up the left foot in front of the right, well pointed and rising on the toes. On the second bar step again sideways with the flat of the right foot and draw up the left behind the right heel. On the third bar step again sideways with the right foot and draw up the left level with right, rising on the toes. On the fourth bar sink the heels, remaining stationary with the feet in the first position. In the counterpart (section 4) the treads, moving leftwards, are made with the left foot.

The Backward Single and Honour : This amounts to a medium reverence and takes four bars. On the first bar step backwards with the left foot without hopping and bend the knees. On the second bar straighten the left knee and point the toe. On the third bar transfer the weight on to the right foot, rising on the toes ; and on the fourth bar, slide up the left foot level with the right and sink the heels.

CORRANTO

(Suitable for the Coranto d'Espagne)

Fitz William Virginal Book.   *Anon.*

LA VOLTA AND THE CORANTO

Corantos.

Stanza 69   What shall I name those current traverses
That on a triple dactyl foot do run
Close by the ground with sliding passages ?
Wherein the dancer greatest praise hath won
Which with best order can all orders shun ;
For everywhere he wantonly must range
And turn and wind with unexpected change.

Lavoltas.

Stanza 70   Yet there is one, the most delightful kind,
A lofty jumping or a leaping round,
When arm in arm two dancers are entwin'd,
And whirl themselves with strict embracements bound,
And still their feet an anapest do sound ;
An anapest is all their music's song,
Whose first two feet are short and third is long.

(*Orchestra*)

CHAPTER VIII

THE ALLEMANDE

THE Allemande was a stately dance, somewhat akin to the Pavan, but with the peculiarity that the singles and doubles were concluded with a *pied en l'air*, suggestive of the " goose step ". In its country of origin its solemn opening strains were followed by a light springy movement in triple time, named in German " Proportz ". In other countries it appears that this effect of lightening the dance was produced by quickening the pace and introducing hops between the steps as in the coranto. This device, employed in the final strain each time it occurs, lends a pleasing variety to the dance.

It became popular in England during the sixteenth century, where it was usually known as " The Almaine " (also spelt Alman and Almayne).

We will turn to Arbeau for a description of this dance in its primitive form.

The Allemande is a dance full of mediocre (i.e. sobre) gravity, and I think that it is one of our most ancient dances since we are descended from the Allemands. You can dance it in company : For, when you have a demoiselle in hand, several others may plant themselves behind you, each one holding his own (partner), and you will dance all together, going forward, and when you wish, retreating, in duple time, with three steps and a grève, or pied en l'air : and when you will have reached the end of the hall, you can turn round while dancing without letting go of your demoiselle, and the other dancers will follow you doing the same thing as they arrive at the end of the hall : And when the players of instruments cease playing this first part, each one stops and converses with his demoiselle ; and you will recommence as before for the second part : And when the third part comes you will dance it in lighter and quicker duple time, and with introducing little hops as in the Courante : This you will easily understand by the tablature ; the which would scarcely be needed, seeing that there is hardly any change in the movements : however in order that you may understand it all more clearly, I will not spare myself the trouble of giving it to you in writing.

The steps of the Allemande, as shown by Arbeau, consist of a sequence of doubles terminated by one pair of singles. The first and second part constitute an odd number of bars, the extra bar being filled by a pair of singles. His light movement has an even number of bars. He sets his tablature to an insipid tune, of the humdrum kind (one of those which sound as though he had invented them on the spot as a convenient framework for his tablature). I have therefore selected a fine sixteenth-century English tune in place of it, since I consider it most important that one should dance to interesting music. This tune also has an odd number of bars in the first strain, which would represent Arbeau's combined first and second parts, and a last strain containing an even number

144

A page from Rawlinson Manuscript.
Bodleian Library.

THE ALLEMANDE

of bars, which by its character lends itself well to the lighter movement, to be played a little faster and with the steps ornamented by hops.

The Figure of the Dance

This consists mainly of a forward movement similar to that of the processional pavan. If it is performed in a hall the dancers may either circle the hall or else alternate the forward and backward movement, in which the backward double would be termed a reprise.

How to Execute the Steps

Each double takes one bar of four beats.

The Doubles : On the first beat, step forward on the flat of the left foot : on the second beat, step forward with the right, rising on the toes : on the third beat, lower the heels and step forward on the flat of the left foot, and on the fourth beat, rising on the toes, perform a right *grève* by kicking forward the right foot, knee high, with the toe well pointed. This *grève* should be done smartly with great precision. The right double is performed in the same manner, using reverse feet.

The Singles : On the first beat, step forward on the flat of the left foot : on the second beat, rising on the left toe, perform a right *grève*. Make the right single in similar fashion, using reverse feet. Hold the body upright and make the movements with great precision and neatness. The Allemande, thus performed, though lacking the sinuous grace of the pavan, yet has its own formal charm, putting one in mind of the popular seventeenth-century tune " Step Stately ".

The Hopped Doubles and Singles : In these, each of the steps is preceded by a hop on the stationary foot which comes a fraction in advance of the beat, whereas the step is made precisely on the beat. There is no hop before the *grève*.

ALLEMANDE

Anon., sixteenth century.

4 doubles: (l.r.l.r.) ....

DANCES OF ENGLAND AND FRANCE

2 singles: (l.r.)   1 double: (l.)   2 singles: (r.l.)   1 double: (r.)   2 singles: (l.r.)

Same order of steps repeated

♩ = 88

4 doubles: (l.r.l.r.) hopped.

2 singles: (l.r.)   1 double: (l.)   2 singles: (r.l.)

1 double: (r.)   2 doubles: (l.r.) ....

THE ALLEMANDE

The Rawlinson manuscript provides us with seven allemandes named as follows :—

1. Cozayne's Almayne.
2. The Old Almayne.
3. Brunswicke.
4. The Quene Almayne.
5. The Newe Almayne.
6. Cynthia Almayne.
7. The Newe Cynthia Alemaine.

The music of numbers 3 and 4 has been preserved in the Fitz William Virginal Book in settings by John Bull and William Byrd. To numbers 2, 5, and 7 I have allotted attractive contemporary tunes agreeing with their individual construction. Numbers 1 and 7 belong to the later type of allemande wherein it approaches the style of the balletto and which is well represented by number 4, " The Newe Almayne ", for which I have chosen a lively, cheerful tune bearing the appropriate title " Allemande Nouvelle ".

Starting therefore with number 2, " The Old Almayne," we find this to agree in principle with Arbeau's version of the dance. Although the directions are brief, as with the processional pavan, the formula is supposed to be repeated a number of times until the dancers have circled the room again and again, or travelled a considerable distance out of doors.

THE OLD ALMAYNE

(1) Two singles and a double forward, both ways.
(2) A double forward hopped, four times.

THE FIGURES OF THE DANCE

The couples form up one behind the other as for a procession. During the first strain they step forward making their two singles and a double, beginning with the left foot and repeating the same beginning with the right foot. This is what is meant by the expression " both ways " in the directions given above. The man holds his partner's left hand in his own right, and they step with smoothness and dignity. During the repeat of the first strain they continue the same sequence of steps. Throughout the second strain and its repeat, the dancers continue to circle the room, but instead of the series of two singles and a double they employ only doubles, the which doubles are hopped as in the light movement of the preceding allemande. As many couples as wish may take part.

THE STEPS

These are performed exactly as in the French allemande described by Arbeau, the only distinction lying in the order of the sequences, which is more regular in the English dance than in the French.

DANCES OF ENGLAND AND FRANCE

ALMAN

FitzWilliam Virginal Book.   Robert Johnson.

THE DUKE OF BRUNSWICKE'S ALMAYNE

(1) A double forward and reprise back twice.
(2) A double forward hopped four times.

THE FIGURES OF THE DANCE

The couples form up one behind the other, as many as wish to take part, facing forward as in the preceding dance. In the first strain they alternately advance and retreat. In the second strain they advance continuously, either

148

circling the room, or coming up the centre and, by means of the turning movement called " conversion ", returning to the starting point. This turning
movement, which should take place during the fourth double, is effected
by the man turning a quarter-turn to the left on his first step, and another
quarter-turn on his second step (which is made backwards), meanwhile guiding
his partner round in a semicircle, so that with the third step they face round
in the opposite direction, the lady still standing on his right. They then proceed
down the room during the repeat of the second strain, turning again during
the fourth double ready to recommence the first strain.

The Steps

The forward doubles and the hopped doubles are performed as in the two
preceding almaynes. The name " reprise " used in this dance, indicates a
retreat, and is merely a backward double, finishing with a *grève*.

THE DUKE OF BRUNSWICKE'S ALMAN

Fitz William Virginal Book. John Bull.

THE QUEEN'S ALMAYNE

SECTION 1. Two singles forward and cast off a double round : two singles sideways, reprise back : twice.

SECTION 2. A double forward hopped four times (repeat).

THE FIGURES OF THE DANCE

The couples form up one behind the other.

First Figure : The two forward singles (*l.* and *r.*) are made advancing hand in hand. The double round is made by all the dancers individually revolving outwardly, the men turning to the left and the women to the right. For this they release hands and make a three-quarter turn by means of the three steps of the double, so as to face one another at the close, ready to perform the pair of sideways singles (*r.* and *l.*). The man holds his partner's right hand in his own and they move in contrary motion. For the reprise, which consists of a right backward double, the dancers face forward again, the man taking his partner's left hand in his own right. This figure is repeated, thus filling the first strain of the music.

Second Figure : An effective way to perform this figure is for the couples to separate, the women in one file, circling to the right, and the men to the left. At the foot of the dance the partners should meet and come up the centre, hand in hand. The first sequence of four doubles brings the leading couple together at the foot of the dance and in the repeat, they advance up the centre to their original position at the head of the dance, the other couples following in their train. This figure occupies strain 2 of the music. The same set of figures is repeated in sections 3 and 4 of the music, and again in sections 5 and 6, which brings the dance to a close.

150

THE ALLEMANDE

The Steps

The steps are performed as in the preceding Allemande except that in place of the *grève* (high kick) a *pied en l'air* (low kick) should be used and the raised foot crossed in front of the stationary foot.

THE QUEEN'S ALMAYNE

Fitz William Virginal Book.

William Byrd.

151

DANCES OF ENGLAND AND FRANCE

Steps as in Section II.

Steps as in Section I.

Steps as in Section II.

152

THE ALLEMANDE

The Newe Almayne

Section 1. A double forward hopped four times.
Section 2. Two singles sideways, a double round : twice.
Section 3. Honour : and one sideways single one after another : a double into your place.
Section 4. Place : one single one after another : a double back into your own places again.

In this dance we have a demonstration of the gradual transformation of the allemande from a stately processional ending with a contrasting light movement, into a kind of balletto beginning with a gay intrada. The only example of the Allemande presented by Cesare Negri in his treatise, *Nuove Inventione di Balli*, shows the development completed ; and the dance is herein called a balletto for four dancers, under the title " Alemana d'Amore ". Early in the seventeenth century, the Allemande went out of use as a dance though persisting as one of the movements of the conventional musical suite.

The Figures of the Dance

First Figure : It transpires from the interplay of movements that " The Newe Almayne " is devised for three couples who make their entry in procession with four hopped doubles. These complete the first strain of the music, at the close of which the partners turn to face one another.

Second Figure : For the two sideways singles each man takes his partner's right hand in his own, as they stand face to face, while they move in contrary motion with left and right singles. For the ensuing left double, still holding right hands, shoulder high, they move round one another and return to their places. This figure is repeated in the reverse direction during which the partners hold left hands, and start with the right foot. This figure occupies the repeat of the first strain of music.

Third Figure : The partners remain face to face and the first couple makes a short reverence after which, turning to face the onlookers, they separate by means of a sideways broken single in contrary directions, the woman making a right single and the man a left. This movement leaves the view open for the second couple. These perform the same movements in turn, separating at the close by means of the sideways broken single (facing the onlookers), so as to leave the view open for the third couple who then perform the same movements. This sequence completed, the partners simultaneously come together again facing one another, by means of a broken double, describing a quarter of a circle inwards. This figure fills the second strain of the music.

Fourth Figure : This figure opens with a gesture called " place ", corresponding with that which Arbeau terms " posture ". This begins at the head of the dance, the first posture being made by the first couple who by contrary motion come together in the centre line. They then separate by means of a broken single. The second couple follow suit and finally the third. The figure closes with a simultaneous broken double describing a half circle inwards, on the last step of which the dancers turn again to face the audience in processional formation. This figure completes the dance in duple time, and occupies the repeat of the second strain of music. There follows in the music a light movement in triple time which forms a delightful finale. This is danced throughout with hops, in saltarello fashion, and the two files of dancers may perform various evolutions, separating and reuniting. I would suggest that in the first strain they cast off (women to the right and men to the left), and proceed down the sides of the room to the foot of the dance, where they unite to come up the centre. The order of the steps throughout the movement should be two broken singles (*l.* and *r.*) and a left broken double, followed by the counterpart of two broken singles (*r.* and *l.*), and a right broken double. Another effective variation would be to make the two singles advancing, and the double turning round each other. When making the left double the man holds his partner's right hand and they turn to the right, the reverse arrangement being adopted for the right double. This figure, halting the progress round the room, should occupy two strains, i.e. the repeat of the first strain and the first time of the second strain. For the repeat of the second, which constitutes the finale of the dance, the couples should circle the room and dance out.

THE STEPS OF THE NEW ALMAYNE

First Movement in Duple Time.

In describing the steps of the opening movement which contains four crotchets to the bar we shall reckon the bar as consisting of two beats, the intervening crotchets being alluded to as the half beats. All the singles and doubles, whether hopped or smooth in the new almayne are " broken " steps (Italian " spezzate ").

Hopped Broken Singles : On the first beat, step forward on the left foot and at the half beat, rising on the toes, bring up the right toe level with the heel of the left foot. On the second beat, step forward a few inches again with the left foot and at the half beat, hop on it, simultaneously raising the right foot forward (*pied en l'air*). Make the right hopped single in the same way, using reverse feet.

Hopped Broken Doubles : These occupy two bars for each double ; we will therefore reckon the two bars together as four beats in describing the double. On the first beat, step forward on the left foot and at the half beat, hop on it. On the second beat, step forward on the right foot, and at the half beat, hop on it. On the third beat, step forward on the left foot and at the half beat, rising on the toes, bring up the right toe level with the left heel. On the fourth beat, step forward a few inches again with the left foot and at the half beat, hop on it, simultaneously raising the right foot forward in a *pied en l'air*. Make the right double in the same way, using reverse feet. It is only in section 1 of the duple time that the steps are hopped ; those in sections 2, 3, and 4 are all smooth.

Smooth Sideways Broken Singles : These occur in sections 2 and 3 : On the first beat, step sideways on the left foot and at the half beat, rising on the toes, bring up the right toe level with the left heel. On the second beat, step again sideways a few inches further on the left foot, simultaneously raising the right foot forward an inch or two from the ground. Make the right sideways single in the same manner, starting with the right foot and moving towards the right.

Smooth Broken Doubles, Advancing or Circling : On the first beat, step forward on the left foot, with an anticipatory bend of the right knee. On the second beat, rising on the toes, step forward with the right. On the third beat, sinking the heels, step again with the left foot and at the half beat, rising on the toes, bring up the right toe level with the left heel. On the fourth beat, sinking the heels, step forward a few inches again with the left foot and raise the right foot forward two inches from the ground. Make the right broken double in the same way, beginning with the right foot.

Honour : This is a half reverence occupying two beats. On the first beat, step backward a few inches with the left foot, bending the knee and inclining the head and body slightly. Throw the weight on to the left foot when you have stepped and straighten the right knee, pointing the toe. On the second beat, restore the weight to the right foot, rising on the toes with straightened knees while you rapidly bring up the left toe level with the right. At the half beat sink the heels. As you sink the heels, turn a quarter turn to the left, for the man, and to the right for the woman. In this manner both partners will land facing the spectators with feet joined in the third position, left and right respectively. The partners who have made the reverence next proceed with the broken sideways single, left for the man and right for the woman, at the close of which the raised foot is lowered beside the other in the first position. The view is thus laid open for the second couple, who go through the same actions and lastly the third. The broken double, by means of which all the dancers return to their own places, curves inwards so that at the close the partners face one another in double file, which brings us to the end of the second strain.

Place : The repeat of the second strain opens with the posture which is herein designated as " place ". To accomplish this, the first man, making a right quarter turn on his right toe, steps with his left foot on to the centre line between the two files, thereby turning his back to the audience. He holds his partner's right hand in his own, shoulder high and, resting the weight of his body on the left foot, extends the right obliquely sideways elegantly pointed. His partner simultaneously performs the same actions, stepping on to the centre line also with her left foot on which she rests while pointing the right obliquely sideways. Thus she faces forward, so that they pose face to face. This posture occupies two beats (one bar) and is followed by a sideways broken single out-wards facing forward. The man anticipates this by making a rapid half turn left on his right toe. His partner is already facing forward and while he makes a left sideways broken single, she makes one to the right at the close of which the raised foot is lowered beside the other in the first position. The view is thus laid open for the second couple to perform the same actions, who are followed in turn by the third couple. The remaining two bars of the strain are filled by the broken double which makes an inward curve, reuniting the partners face to face in double file as in the preceding figure. This closes the movement in duple time; there should therefore be a final chord during which the partners salute one another with the half reverence called " honour ". The dancers then make a quarter turn (men left and women right), so as to face forward for the light movement in triple time. In this movement the steps are hopped and follow the regular order of two singles and a double, alternately left and right, throughout. The music, being in light triple time, will comprise one accented beat to the bar; that which corresponds with the *half* beat in the duple time movement will be relegated to the third beat of the bar, and will be called the " off beat " for the sake of clarity in describing the steps in detail.

Hopped Broken Singles in Triple Time : These occupy two bars each : On the first beat, step forward on the left foot and on the off beat, rising on the toes, bring up the right toe level with the left heel. On the second beat, step forward again a few inches on the left foot and on the off beat, hop on it, simultaneously raising the right foot forward an inch or two from the ground. Make the right hopped broken single in the same way, beginning with the right foot.

Hopped Broken Doubles in Triple Time : These occupy four bars each. On the first beat, step forward on the left foot, and on the off beat, hop on it. On the second beat, step forward with the right foot and on the off beat, hop on it. On the third beat, step forward on the left foot and on the off beat, rising on the toes, bring up the right toe level with the left heel. On the fourth beat, step forward again a few inches on the left foot and on the off beat, hop on it, simultaneously raising the right foot forward an inch or two from the ground. Make the right hopped broken double in the same way, starting with the right foot.

In the sixteenth century Italian treatises the broken singles are called " spezzate " and the broken doubles " seguite spezzate ".

Arm Movements : In making the short reverence called " honour ", as you step backward with the left foot, draw the right arm leftwards across the body, bent at the elbow (with the hand a little raised), and draw the left arm back bent outward from the elbow. As you restore the weight to the right foot, bring forward the left arm to meet the right with hands bent inward and upward, afterwards moving the arms from the elbow downward and outward.

THE ALLEMANDE

In general let the arms move gently to left and right, keeping the upper arm low but moving freely in harmony with the body movements. In making the posture, wherein the partners stand on the centre line face to face with clasped right hands, shoulder high, the left arm should be lowered, and curved gracefully outwards.

ALLEMANDE NOUVELLE

Clavier Tablature Book of Bernard Schmid,
Strasburg, 1577.

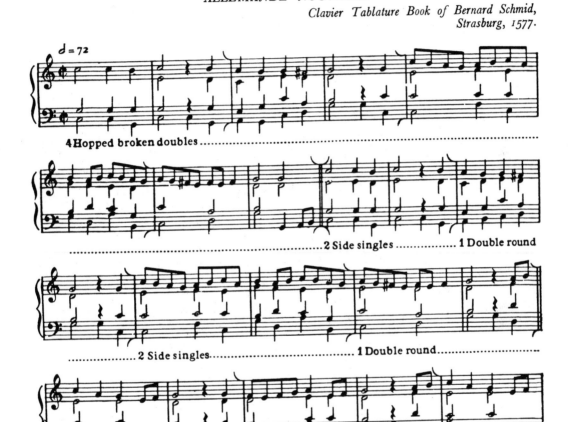

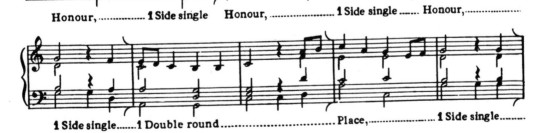

157

DANCES OF ENGLAND AND FRANCE

Place, ... 1 Side single   Place, ... 1 Side single   1 Double into own places

PROPORTIO IN SALTARELLO

Grace in dancing.

Stanza 73　These various forms of dancing Love did frame
And besides these a hundred million mo ;
And as he did invent, he taught the same
With goodly gesture and with comely show,
Now keeping state, now humbly honouring low.
And ever for the persons and the place
He taught most fit and best according grace.

Concord.　　　　　*　　*　　*　　*

Stanza 112　What if by often interchange of place
Sometimes the woman gets the upper hand ?
That is but done for more delightful grace,
For on that part she doth not ever stand ;
But, as the measure's law doth her command,
She wheels about and ere the dance doth end
Into her former place she doth transcend.

(*Orchestra*)

CHAPTER IX

CONCLUSION

Retenez cette Vérité
 Vous qui du goût cherchez les traces :
L'Esprit, les Talents, La Beauté,
 Rien ne réussit sans les Graces.

THE dances described in this treatise have the quality of spontaneity, which exercises a subtle fascination, alike on the performers and the onlookers. They are beautiful and their music is beautiful. The two go hand in hand ; for fine music whether it be folk music or cultivated music, inspires the dancer and is truly recreative, thus producing an invigorating effect of gaiety, happiness, and contentment.

I once heard it stated at a demonstration of English folk dancing that there was no need for the participants to be *graceful*. The speaker, as it happened, was both graceful and skilled in that particular style of dancing ; and I conclude that the remark was rather intended to reassure and persuade the more timid to come and join the dance ! It seems natural that most people should prefer when dancing, even though it be purely for social diversion, to be shown how to bear themselves in a manner that is comely and pleasing. Moreover, there are many ways and degrees of being graceful, depending largely on one's physical attributes ; yet when a dance is well and neatly performed with easy movements of arms and body in harmony with those of the feet (the object thereof being largely one of balance), there emerges a kind of natural, unconscious grace that is satisfying to the eye. This satisfaction is increased where there is sensitiveness to the music and the music itself is interesting. Gesture should in most cases be moderate. The hands, especially a man's, look well either half closed, or slightly rounded, and there are occasions when the man's disengaged hand may be placed lightly on the hip, an effect which came about naturally when the left hand was laid on the hilt of the sword in a lively dance to prevent it from swinging about. Where the arm is gently waved to and fro, this is usually done from the elbow downwards, the upper arm being carried lowered but *not* pressed against the body. These waving movements also produce a symmetrical effect to counterbalance the action of the hips and feet.

The attractions of a good dancer are very individual, as happens with any other art, some excelling in one style and others in another, according to their physical and mental qualities. Equally varied is the pleasure to be had from watching different types of dancing, the outcome of diverse traditions and racial

159

ideals. We can enjoy seeing the Lancashire clog dancers, the cockney heel and toe experts, the magnificent Highland exponents of reels, flings, and sword dances, overflowing with vitality ; and we can be dazzled by the vivacity of the skilled Irish performers of hornpipes, double jigs, and rants. The Irish dancers, however, unlike the Highlanders (so free of gesture), frequently keep their arms lowered and held close to the body ; but this arises from the fact that their art is centred in the footwork, which exhibits such prodigious speed and intricacy that the eyes of the beholders are entirely focussed thereon. With the modern Spanish stage dancer, although the work of the feet is skilful and exquisitely controlled, the interest lies rather in the superb poses of the figure, the responsive arm movements, the wide range of facial expression and the bewildering rhythmic flow of the castanets. Indian dancers, whose traditions date back into a far-off antiquity, employ their supple bodies in movements whose rippling motions can best be likened to those of serpents, birds, and other creatures of the wild. Ethiopians in their exuberance and Tibetans in their mystic exaltation perform astounding acrobatics, interspersed freely with speech and song ! Dancers of the extreme Orient, on the other hand, carry their dancing upwards from hip and torso, through the head and shoulders and along the arms to the finger-tips. Indeed, they may be said to dance with their hands, whose fingers have the flexibility and softness of flowering grasses. I can remember being taken in 1882–83 to that unforgettable exhibition, called "The Japanese Village" ; and in the little theatre which was one of its many attractions, gazing in wonder at the Japanese dancers. These, in their robes of turquoise, jade, pink-ruby, and topaz stood rooted to the spot, swaying, writhing, and swirling like the lilies of the field stirred by frolicsome breezes. I was suddenly recalled to my senses by the scornful comments of our cockney nurse, as she exclaimed indignantly " Call that dancing ! That ain't dancing ! Why they never even *moved* their feet ! " Well, for me all kinds of dancing make their appeal, except the purely grotesque, the sinister, and the over-stylized.

And what, apart from its fresh simplicity (grave or gay), constitutes the charm of the renaissance dances of England and France ? It is their undulating character, produced by the anticipatory bendings of knee and instep, with subsequent " raising of the bodye " (as Coplande expresses it),[1] suggestive of dancing wavelets over a tranquil sea ; and also the gentle advancing of the hip on the side of the stepping foot, so aptly likened to the deploying gesture of the peacock, and the sprightly hops and leaps with interchanges of salutations, resembling the courting of butterflies. This pliancy of knee, ankle, and instep, and even toes demands supple, flat-heeled shoes and cannot be satisfactorily accomplished by those who wear stiff-soled or high-heeled shoes. Once I saw a portion of a film, showing popular dancing in Seville on the occasion of an annual festival. I was interested to observe traces of these dipping and

[1] The Manner to dance bace dances (Appendix to *French Grammer* (1521), Bodleian Library).

CONCLUSION

rising movements, formerly considered indispensable to fine dancing. This would not apply to those outdoor peasant dances in which sabots are worn, where the attraction lies in their rhythmic clicking, alluded to by Arbeau as " un bruit gracieux ".

I have endeavoured throughout this work to convey in clear, precise language all the requisite information to those who may desire to reproduce these dances ; and have made use of frequent reiterations, at the risk of tediousness, in order to avoid for students the distraction caused by hunting up details in earlier chapters. In the hope that I have thereby placed the results of my past researches easily within their grasp, and by correlating such with my own practical experience have made " these dry bones live ", I will now take leave of my readers with cordial good wishes for their future success in this field of art.

The speech of Love :—of other things upon the earth.

Stanza 55   *See how those flowers, that have sweet beauty too*
(The only jewels that the earth doth wear,
When the young sun in bravery her doth woo)
As oft as they the whistling wind do hear,
Do wave their tender bodies here and there ;
And though their dance no perfect measure is
Yet oftentimes their music makes them kiss.

     *   *   *   *

Stanza 96   Lo, this is Dancing's true nobility,
Dancing, the child of Music and of Love ;
Dancing, itself both love and harmony,
Where all agree and all in order move ;
Dancing, the art that all arts do approve ;
The fair character of the world's consent,
The heaven's true figure and th' earth's ornament.

Stanzas chosen from *Orchestra, or a Poem of Dancing* (by Sir John Davies, c. 1594)

BIBLIOGRAPHY

MS. of MARIE DE BOURGOGNE, C. 1450. *Plusieurs basses danses.*

MICHEL TOULOUZE, C. 1486. *L'art et Instruction de bien Dancer.*

ANON., fifteenth century. *Manuscrit de Bayeux.*

JOAN AMBROSIO DALZA, 1508. *Intabulatura di Lauto, Libro Quarto.*

ROBERT COPLANDE, 1521. *The Manner of Dancing Bace Dances.*

PIERRE ATTAIGNANT, 1529. *Dixhuit Basses Dances.*

    ,,   ,,   1530. *Quatorze Gaillardes neuf Pavennes, etc.*

SIR THOMAS ELYOT, 1531. *The Govenour.*[1]

ANTONIUS DE ARENA, 1536. *Ad Suos Compagnones, qui sunt de persona friantes ; Bassas Dansas & Branlos praticantes, etc.*

ANON., 1570. *Rawlinson Manuscript.*

FABRITIO CAROSO, 1581. *Il Ballarino.*

THOINOT ARBEAU,[2] 1588. *Orchésographie.*

SIR JOHN DAVIES, 1594. *Orchestra or a Poem of Dancing.*[3]

THOMAS MORLEY, 1597. *A Plaine and Easie Introduction to Practicall Musicke.*

FABRITIO CAROSO, 1600. *Nobilita dei Dame.*

ANON., C. 1610. *Dolmetsch Lute Manuscript.*

CESARE NEGRI, 1604. *Nuove Inventioni di Balli.*

WILLIAM SHAKESPEARE. *Much Ado About Nothing* and *Henry VIII.*

THOMAS MACE, 1687. *Music's Monument.*

AURELIO CAPMANY, 1931. *El Baile y la Danza.*

P. D. OUSPENSKY, 1938. *A New Model of the Universe.*[4]

1. Republished, Everyman's Library.
2. Anagram for Jehan Tabourot.
3. Republished, Chatto and Windus.
4. Published, Routledge and Kegan Paul, Ltd.

INDEX